'The House v Weather was Made'

A BIOGRAPHY OF CHAMBERLAIN'S HIGHBURY

C000056200

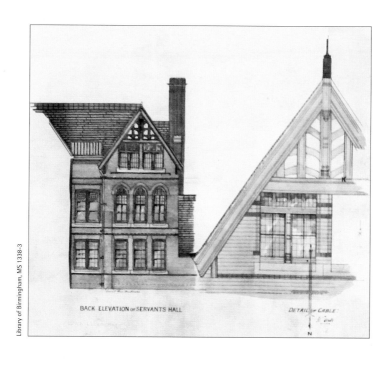

Library of Birmingham, MS 1338-3

BACK ELEVATION of SERVANTS HALL

DETAIL of GABLE

PETER MARSH WITH JUSTINE PICK

Published by West Midlands History Limited

Minerva Mill Innovation Centre, Alcester, Warwickshire, UK.

© 2019 West Midlands History Limited.

© All images are copyright as credited.

The rights of Peter Marsh and Justine Pick to be identified as authors of this work have been asserted by them in accordance with the Copyright, Designs and Patents Act 1988.

All rights reserved. No part of this publication may be reproduced, stored in a retrieval system, or transmitted, in any form or by any means, electronic, mechanical, photocopying, recording, or otherwise, without the prior permission of West Midlands History Limited. This book is sold subject to the condition that it shall not, by way of trade or otherwise, be lent, re-sold, hired or otherwise circulated without the publisher's prior consent in any form of binding or cover other than that in which it is published and without a similar condition including this condition being imposed on the subsequent purchaser.

ISBN: 978-1-905036-72-1

Cover image: House: Library of Birmingham from Warwickshire Photographic Survey.
Chamberlain family: © Cadbury Research Library: Special Collections.

Caric Press Limited, Merthyr Tydfil, Wales.

To Joseph Chamberlain's civic vision

Contents

Introduction
THE SEATS OF POLITICAL POWER

Highbury remains unique among the historic seats of political power in Great Britain. It was not the palace of a king such as ruled Britain until the seventeenth century. It was not a stately home or great country house like those of the aristocracy and landed gentry who governed the kingdom into the nineteenth century. Nor was it in London where the governing elite maintained houses near Parliament. It stood on the suburban outskirts of a metal-manufacturing town.

Highbury was built and landscaped to help Joseph Chamberlain, an industrialist who had become a Radical reformer in Birmingham, to make his power effective at the national level. And in this he was successful. Within a decade of its construction, Highbury had become synonymous with Chamberlain as one of the most influential men in British politics alongside the alternating prime ministers, Lord Salisbury at Hatfield and Gladstone at Hawarden, and the Whig leader, the Duke of Devonshire at Chatsworth.

Highbury was also unique in another way. Chamberlain made more direct political use of the estate than Salisbury, Gladstone and the Duke of Devonshire did of their great houses. All these men brought their close confidants together at their homes. But Chamberlain used Highbury also to rally his electoral support, and sometimes he used these rallies to address the country at large on issues of urgent national concern.

But the world which these men led was fundamentally changed by the First World War of 1914 to 1918. That war shattered the integrated trading system that had spread across Europe since the middle of the nineteenth century, and it also undermined the economic value of landed estates. In doing so, it ended the era of great homes as power-houses in Britain. The change was symbolised after the First World War by the gift of Chequers, a country house not far from London, for use by the serving Prime Minister on the assumption that political leaders were no longer likely to own such a place themselves.

Highbury was particularly vulnerable to this change. Joseph Chamberlain made little provision after his death for the maintenance of Highbury, unlike the stately homes inherited by Lord Salisbury and the Duke of Devonshire. It has managed to survive only because of a lingering gospel of dedication to the civic service that inspired its construction.

The proposal to tell this story was originally made by Mike Gibbs, the generous promoter of West Midlands history. Mike secured the services of Justine Pick as research assistant for this project; and she proved to be so much more. She not only worked her way through the voluminous correspondence of Joseph Chamberlain's third wife, Mary, to her mother in Massachusetts, which provides an intimate account of life at Highbury. Justine entered imaginatively into the story she uncovered, and brought out dimensions that were previously unrecognised. This study is also heavily reliant on Phillada Ballard's detailed examination and dedication to the restoration of the gardens and parkland that form an essential part of the Highbury estate. Phillada is a vital member of the Chamberlain Highbury Trust recently constituted to re-establish Highbury on a flourishing and enduring basis. This book is dedicated to the civic vision that underlies that Trust.

Chapter One
THE FOUNDING PURPOSE

Highbury was designed and constructed to promote the political purposes of Joseph Chamberlain. While he may be a distant memory in Birmingham and Britain today, at the end of the nineteenth century he was, as Winston Churchill recalled, 'incomparably the most live, sparkling, insurgent, compulsive figure in British affairs'. The first statesman to be universally known by his nickname, '"Joe" was the one who made the weather'. And he made it at Highbury.

No one envisaged a great role in public life for Joseph Chamberlain when he was a young man. The eldest son of a prosperous shoe manufacturer in the City of London, Joseph received the best education available for someone of unorthodox religious background – the Chamberlains were Unitarian – to prepare him for a career in industry. At the age of seventeen he was sent to Birmingham to look after a large investment his father had made in the metal manufacture of wood screws.

Until he turned thirty Joseph concentrated his talents on transforming this family business into one of the triumphs of Victorian industry. The company accelerated its production and marketing of screws of all sorts to create a UK-wide monopoly; it extended its market throughout continental Europe and across the Atlantic, and established the terms of the trade worldwide.

Involvement in this business alerted Joseph to a parallel set of social needs and consequences – needs and consequences that had to be addressed in the public arena. Chamberlain was one of the first industrialists in Birmingham to recognise the need for an educated workforce to secure more cooperative relations with labour and increase the economic dividends to all concerned. However, he was rare among Birmingham manufacturers in also discerning the harmful social consequences of the great factories that were being built for mass production. Birmingham prided itself on its comparative social tranquillity which was based on close relations between masters and men in small workshops. It needed Chamberlain to point out to the British Association that when it came to Birmingham in 1866, '[a revolution] is taking place in the principal hardware trades, and is … depriving [the town] of its special characteristic, viz. the number of its small manufacturers, which has hitherto materially influenced its social and commercial prosperity as well as its politics'.

That social pronouncement coincided with another momentous statement – this time by George Dawson, an unorthodox Baptist minister, at the opening of the Library of Birmingham in 1866. Dawson declared: 'A great town exists to discharge towards the people of that town, the duties that a great nation exists to discharge towards the people of that nation – that a town exists here by the grace of God, that a great town is a solemn organisation through which should flow, and in which should be shaped, all the highest, loftiest, and truest ends of man's intellectual and moral nature.' Dawson's declaration and Chamberlain's warning gave rise to what came to be known as the Civic Gospel. Dawson pointed to the institution through which Birmingham could address the social concerns to which Chamberlain drew attention: the hitherto disparaged Town Council. Chamberlain took Dawson's message to heart and directed his attention increasingly to the concerns of the town.

He began by attempting to place responsibility for the provision of elementary education in the hands of England's towns and cities. He played a leading part in the formation by Birmingham industrialists of a National Education League to secure the necessary legislation from Parliament. This concern led him to become a member of the Town Council. The reluctance of Parliament and the ratepayers of Birmingham to accept all the demands of the National Education League deepened Chamberlain's commitment to a Radical agenda for town and country. When progressive forces gained control of the Town Council in 1873, they installed Chamberlain as mayor. He promptly embarked upon a programme of reform which turned Birmingham within less than three years into a widely applauded model of industrial city government. He sold the Chamberlain interest in the family firm to their cousins, the Nettlefolds, at a profit that enabled him to devote the rest of his life to public service.

However, the death in 1875 of his wife Florence, with whom he had worked closely in developing his political agenda, shook his sense of purpose. He regained it by shifting his focus away from the civic venues they had both loved and on to the national arena. A year after the death of Florence, Chamberlain secured election as a

Member of Parliament for Birmingham and resigned his mayoralty though not his place on the Town Council. Fiercely ambitious, he strove to place himself in a national position similar to but strikingly different from the great leaders of his day. They came primarily from the landed classes. He was a 'prince of industry' representing one of the heartlands of industry in the world's first industrial nation.

To realise that ambition he required a mansion greater than the home he had built for his family near the centre of Birmingham in Edgbaston. He turned to the man who had established himself as the architect of the Civic Gospel, John Henry Chamberlain, not a relative of Joe but a member of his inner circle and of Dawson's congregation. J.H. Chamberlain drew his inspiration from John Ruskin who saw in Gothic architecture a fusion of social purpose and the irregularity of nature, a fusion readily adaptable to the practical social and political aspirations of the Civic Gospel. J.H. Chamberlain's vision found its most fitting expression in the elementary school buildings that sprang up across industrial Birmingham at the urging of Joseph Chamberlain's National Education League. Their polychromatic ventilation towers formed the aspirational spires of Birmingham, bringing health and learning to the crowded tenements of the town. Joseph asked John Henry Chamberlain to design a house permeated with the ideals of the Civic Gospel and appropriate to Joe's national aspirations.

The surroundings of the new mansion would be as important as its architecture. Joe wanted more space than Edgbaston allowed, but he also insisted that the new estate remain identified with Birmingham. He knew that a generous stretch of land could be purchased on the southwestern fringe of Birmingham, looking out to the Worcestershire countryside. And it was close to the train station at Kings Heath which could carry him into the heart of Birmingham and on to Westminster. He could return readily at weekends during the parliamentary year to develop the gardening that he had come to love in Edgbaston, and now he could do so on a greater scale. Both house and gardens would give him ample space to gather together his political friends and rally the popular forces around them.

Though impressive, the new house and gardens still lacked the element of ostentation that Joe knew he needed to make his mark. No one could accuse Britain's governing aristocracy of understatement in the stately homes that displayed their wealth and power. Joseph Chamberlain could not match that. However, he found what he sought in a line of glasshouses stretching from the new Drawing Room – eventually twenty-five of them – where he could cultivate and display exotic plants, particularly the orchids that became his trademark.

John Henry gave Joseph some of his best work imbued with the spirit that inspired them both. Though both men acted promptly, the house was not quite ready in the spring of 1880 when Joseph, having mobilised electoral support for the Liberal party, pushed his way into Gladstone's second ministry as President of the Board of Trade. Less than four years after his election to Parliament, he was already a major player on the national stage.

He positioned the house at the highest northern edge of the sweep of land he had purchased on the fringe of Birmingham looking south towards the Lickey Hills. He called it Highbury, the name with a nice ring to it of the district in London where he spent his youth. The house was built in local red brick with white stone ornamentation. J.H. Chamberlain punctuated its south front with one of his favourite compositional strategies drawn from the Gothic love of irregularity: three tall but dissimilar gables to left, right and centre, as in his finest design, the School of Art, completed before his untimely death two years after the opening of Highbury. Though Highbury was the most imposing house yet constructed for any of the industrial elite of Birmingham, Joe's supporters did not find it pretentious. He had not abandoned the environs of their town. When the wind blew from the northwest, you could still detect smoke from the factories of Selly Oak.

But the predominant impression Highbury made on its residents and visitors was of a large estate in the country rather than in the suburbs of a major industrial city. Thirty acres of garden and fields, eventually extended to one hundred, stretched out in front of the house, all beautifully landscaped when the house finally opened. Alongside J.H. Chamberlain as architect, Joe had commissioned Edward Milner, a renowned landscape gardener, to take the Highbury estate in hand. Milner had already worked with Joe in landscaping his home in Edgbaston. And Joe was himself by now an experienced gardener with decided if somewhat old-fashioned views. In gardens, unlike politics, Joe disliked hard straight lines, and in gardening outside he preferred English flowers like buttercups and roses to the exotics he cultivated in his glasshouses.

The basic Milner plan for the landscape allowed for the addition of features that Joe designed. A straight terrace stretched along the front of the house, providing an elevated platform from which Joe could address assemblies of his supporters. The entrance to the gardens below lay a short way to the west of the house and continued in a series of paths and beds that wound gently down the slope. The house disappeared from view as one came upon a lake large enough for boating and fishing. The visitor approached it over a rustic bridge which Milner had designed, with a boathouse nearby and a summerhouse in the background. Milner also transformed a clay pit beside an old oak off the main circuit path into an upper pool with a bench that Joe found particularly restful. Eighteen acres were turned over to farmland to meet the needs of the household with fruit, vegetables and pasturage for meat and milk production. The farmland added to the attractiveness of the landscape with all the field flowers Joe loved: poppies, buttercups and cornflowers. Extended and elaborated throughout the rest of Joe's active career, the gardens and farmland of Highbury conveyed the impression of a thousand acres instead of a hundred.

It was the gardens that his children loved most in their new home. They had treasured their moments with their father in the gardens of their Edgbaston home, where he encouraged them to take charge of small sections. But the thirteen bedrooms in their new house made clear that it was not designed primarily for family purposes. He introduced the younger ones to Highbury at their request in the autumn of 1879 when it was still very much under construction. Beatrice, Austen and Neville were away – Beatrice at a finishing school in Fontainebleau, Austen and Neville at Rugby. Their little sisters, Florence, Hilda and Ethel, ranging in age from five to eight, were overawed by but immensely proud of their eminent and usually distant father, and they accompanied him out quickly to see how the gardening was taking shape.

It was not until the summer of 1881, a year after Highbury was fully opened, that it was used for the public purposes for which it was designed. Joe threw the house and grounds open for a rally by the Junior Liberal Association of Birmingham to strengthen its forces and clear off the debt it had incurred to improve its premises in the town.

They were accompanied by their senior supporters and leading practitioners of the Civic Gospel: R.W. Dale and H.W. Crosskey, the Dissenting ministers who were its foremost preachers, the president of the Liberal Association and its main national organiser, aldermen and members of the Town Council, with J.H. Chamberlain on hand to show the gathering over his handiwork. All but Joe, who remained in London to face a mounting crisis in Ireland with which the Cabinet had to deal.

The young Liberals of Birmingham responded enthusiastically to the welcome to his home. More than a thousand turned up for the event, most arriving on chartered buses. They were shown into the grounds, many were shown over the house, and the most privileged were shown into Joe's study which looked out over the terrace and garden. They discovered, according to a detailed report in the supportive *Birmingham Daily Post* (11 July 1881), that what they considered 'the comparatively modest exterior of the house afforded little indication of the splendid appearance of the interior'. Here, particularly in the upward soaring, top-lit two-storey central Hall, J.H. Chamberlain conveyed the ambitions of his patron effectively. Papered in costly fabric with corniced ceilings all with the naturalistic patterning beloved by Ruskin's disciples, the interior of Highbury exuded cultured affluence and high aspiration.

Throughout the house the visitors were struck by its luxurious elegance. Guided by J.H. Chamberlain, they noted that the floor of the central Hall was 'of polished wood, after the style generally adopted on the Continent, and seen to perfection in some of the French chateaux', and was 'nearly covered in a rich Turkey carpet … On one side is an arcade formed of three Gothic arches, supported by marble pillars, and in the recesses are handsome vases each containing a palm or fern. The walls are richly ornamented with … carved oak and inlaid wood, and here and there fixed carved oak cases containing choice specimens of porcelain.' Those 'allowed to take a peep' at the library where Joe worked noted its 'oak shelves with handsome carvings' and ceiling panelled in 'beautifully inlaid wood'. They were more impressed by the boudoir of the chatelaine of the house, currently Joe's youngest sister Clara, its walls 'draped with a delicately-coloured tapestry to within about eighteen inches of the ceiling', leaving space for 'a frieze upon which are painted figures in antique style, and a beautifully-coloured cornice'. They passed on into the drawing room 'decorated in princely style', then the spacious conservatory with a marble fountain edged with ferns and foliage plants, and finally a hundred feet of heated glasshouses 'crowded with choice plants and flowers', beginning with one devoted to orchids from the East Indies. They emerged from the corridor of glasshouses into the gardens, one path leading to the rose garden, another between shrubberies and flower beds towards a small pool for aquatic plants and on to the larger pond crossed by rustic bridges.

Then, seated on the lawn in front of the house, they watched the afternoon's entertainment, beginning with 'operatic and other popular music' performed by a military band. Bows, arrows and targets were provided to the right of the lawn as an alternative for those who wished to try their skill at archery. After the band music, the Birmingham Athletic Club put on a display of exercises on the parallel bars, Indian clubs, heavy weights, storming boards and horizontal bars. The festivities concluded with a choir and a number of songs.

Though built to handle such an event, this inauguration of Highbury as a venue for large-scale political purposes was extraordinary. More than half a decade would pass before Highbury would attract the kind of attention that Joe and his architect intended. Only within the confines of Birmingham did Joe yet have that eminence. When Conservative critics there censured Highbury for charging two shillings and sixpence for admission to the Junior Liberal rally when admission to the home of the Duke of Devonshire at Chatsworth was free, they exaggerated the heights to which Joe had risen nationally. Highbury in the early 1880s was still of essentially local significance. Joe used it, as he had his home in Edgbaston, for small dinner gatherings of local allies and hospitality for close associates up from London. Otherwise, with strong local support, he left his Birmingham base to look after itself.

His elevation to the Cabinet less than four years after his election to Parliament, though swift, was to an office of low rank. He conceived of himself as leader of the Liberal party's Radical left. Even there, however, he was rivalled by his friend Sir Charles Dilke. And neither man possessed as yet the political weight and eminence of Lord Hartington, heir to the Duchy of Devonshire and leader of the large Whig faction within the government. These men jockeyed for advantage over the next five years, jealously scrutinised by Gladstone as Prime Minister.

Joe meanwhile welcomed opportunities to strengthen his standing in London away from reminders of the tragedy that had befallen him with the death of Florence. Upon appointment to the Cabinet and before Highbury opened, he acquired a house in a fashionable quarter of London close to the new Albert Hall. He used it to strengthen his relationships at Westminster with small dinners, as he had in Birmingham. He also enjoyed his reception in the glittering upper echelons of parliamentary society which welcomed a handsome and sparkling conversationalist to their midst.

By comparison, the atmosphere at Highbury was sobering. Its chatelaines, Clara and then Joe's eldest child Beatrice, were serious young women proud of Birmingham's commitment to the Civic Gospel but ill at ease when their responsibilities took them to London's West End. Joe was on the lookout for a woman who would function well in both worlds. He thought he might have found her in the philosopher Herbert Spencer's secretary, Beatrice Potter, who figured in Westminster society. She certainly fell under Joe's spell, but she found his demand for subservience of mind intolerable and ultimately married Sidney Webb.

Even if Joe became a serious contender for the highest positions in national politics, without a vivacious hostess Highbury would remain a backwater in the surrounding social world. The things Highbury lacked to satisfy Joe's aspirations for the estate would be supplied after the Liberal party split over Gladstone's proposal to give Ireland Home Rule. But paradoxically this development destroyed Joe's chance to lead the party as a whole.

Chapter Two
FRUSTRATED HOPES

As President of the Board of Trade Joe had hoped to remove social evils nationally, thereby emulating his mayoralty achievement in providing Birmingham with affordable clean water. The only *Punch* cartoon (22 March 1884) that he kept in a place of honour in Highbury for the rest of his life depicted him in the unlikely guise of a little angel, 'The Cherub', taking care of a merchant sailor on a vessel insured for more than three times its commercial worth. This practice of over-insurance was used by unscrupulous ship owners to send unseaworthy vessels out with a full crew of sailors who were unaware that the owners would reap more profit if the sailors died at sea than if they delivered their cargo safely to port. Outraged, Joe attacked the industry as a whole, failing to distinguish between bad ship owners who behaved in this way and the good owners who did not. This indiscriminate attack roused the whole industry against him and thus held up enactment of his Merchant Shipping Bill.

Joe's hard-hitting rhetoric heightened his political salience. In campaigning for a great increase in the working-class electorate in face of opposition from the House of Lords, he likened the Conservative leader there, Lord Salisbury, to the Biblical 'flowers of the field that toil not neither do they spin, yet Solomon in all his glory was not arrayed like one of these'. Salisbury retaliated by carrying his campaign onto Joe's home ground. Joe responded by inviting the rising Liberal star, Lord Rosebery, to speak alongside him in the Town Hall in support of franchise extension. Afterwards Rosebery stayed with Joe at Highbury – the house was beginning to fulfil its intended function.

However, Joe's emotive rhetoric proved counterproductive. The Liberal government put Joe's Merchant Shipping Bill off until they could secure extension of the electorate, in effect until after the next general election. To make sure of a Liberal victory then, Chamberlain appealed to the new working-class voters in a speech about the erosion of natural or common rights which had occurred to the benefit of the rights of private property. 'What ransom', he asked, 'will property pay for the security it enjoyed?'

'Ransom' suggested brigandage rather than social justice. Joe immediately recognised the need to tone down his language, but he was too late to remove the fear it had aroused.

In the ensuing general election the Liberals failed to win the commanding majority he expected. They remained much the largest party in the House of Commons, with eighty-six MPs more than the Conservatives. But that was exactly the number of Irish Nationalists who won election to the Commons under the new franchise. This result threw the Act of Union of 1800 between Great Britain and Ireland into question. That question, the Irish Question, split the Liberal party and drove them from effective power for the next twenty-five years.

No one carried more responsibility for that result than Joseph Chamberlain. First, however, it sharply reduced his hopes of national leadership and drove him back upon his base in Birmingham. Even there he had to fight for his political life.

The outcome of the general election encouraged Gladstone to propose a measure of self-government or 'Home Rule for Ireland', sufficiently generous to secure the support of the Nationalist leader Parnell. Gladstone's Irish proposals were too generous for Chamberlain whose primary concern, in line with the Civic Gospel in Birmingham, was to empower the government, national as well as local, to address the needs of Britain's now fully industrial economy. The Liberal Party, however, brought together an uneasy alliance of aristocratic Whigs, religious Dissenters, free traders and other spokesmen for the middle classes, trade union leaders and progressive advocates for the working classes. Their bond of unity, if they had one, was of respectful devotion to their ageing leader, Gladstone. Chamberlain's disagreement with the Home Rule Bill aroused suspicion that he aimed to dethrone the 'Grand Old Man' of British politics.

Chamberlain owed his rapid rise into the Cabinet to his alliance with Gladstone in turning the Liberals' well-organised electoral base in Birmingham into the National Federation of Liberal Associations that carried the party to victory in 1880. The chief organiser of the Birmingham Liberals, Francis Schnadhorst, had come to resent Chamberlain's high-handed treatment of his home base. As the party split asunder over the Home Rule Bill, Schnadhorst transferred his allegiance to

Gladstone, and the National Federation followed suit. Chamberlain was hard-pressed to carry even Birmingham with him but eventually pulled off a comprehensive victory there.

The significance of that victory was enhanced by the defeat of the Home Rule Bill in the House of Commons and the ensuing general election. Here again Chamberlain and the representation of Birmingham proved of crucial importance. Conservatives and Whig followers of Lord Hartington in the House of Commons joined forces to oppose the Home Rule Bill, but they were not numerous enough to defeat it. Chamberlain and his small band of what now became known as Radical Unionists could make the difference, but only if they won endorsement from the other famous MP from Birmingham, John Bright. As doughty champion of free trade, Bright commanded reverence among Liberals second only to that for Gladstone. Chamberlain's deployment of an endorsement he secured from Bright persuaded enough otherwise uneasy Radical opponents of the Home Rule Bill in the Commons to defeat it.

Birmingham only increased in importance in the ensuing general election. By calling the general election after defeat in the House of Commons, Gladstone turned Irish Home Rule into the defining issue of the electoral contest, with dire consequences for the Liberals because it sharply divided them. The Liberals of Birmingham were more concerned about holding their party together than about the discontents of Ireland, a tide of sentiment that Chamberlain turned to his advantage. Nationally, however, the issue of Irish Home Rule drove its Liberal opponents towards the Conservatives. Gladstone's concentration on Ireland also aroused the hitherto dormant sentiments of democratic imperialism to which Chamberlain gave resonant voice.

This mixture of sentiments combined to turn Birmingham into the electoral pivot of Great Britain and Highbury into the town's power centre. Chamberlain's supporters and allies won all seven constituencies in the town, in one case by a margin of four to one. Nowhere else in the kingdom was the outcome for the Gladstonians so bad. Even so, the swing against them nationally amounted to a landslide. The Conservatives were the main beneficiaries of the swing. They replaced the Liberals as much the largest party in the House of Commons but were still short of a majority. This result made them dependent upon the surprisingly large number of successful Liberal Unionists – 79 in all, including a Radical minority led by Chamberlain from Highbury. The outcome of the general election also added an imperial dimension to the appeal of his Civic Gospel and eventually turned Highbury into a point of pilgrimage for advocates and emissaries of the British Empire.

However, this benign outcome for Chamberlain still lay in the future. In the immediate wake of the election he found himself in an acutely uncomfortable position. Only in Birmingham could he feel tolerably secure. All the key players at Westminster with whom Joe would have to work were either alienated from him or unnatural allies. Gladstone had intensified the sense among the vast majority of Liberals that Chamberlain had betrayed them. John Morley, who had been Chamberlain's closest colleague before the rupture over Home Rule, was now Gladstone's leading lieutenant on Irish issues. Salisbury, as leader of the Conservative Party, offered to serve under the Whig Lord Hartington in a coalition ministry but only if Chamberlain were to be excluded from it. Hartington embodied everything that Chamberlain found dispiriting about the Whig approach to government. However, Hartington had retained his seat in the House of Commons as representative of industrial Lancashire only because Chamberlain had campaigned to give him Radical support. In order to deal with these contending pressures during the formation of a new government, Chamberlain kept his distance from Westminster and remained resolutely in Highbury.

The only leading light on the parliamentary stage who wanted to forge a close relationship with Chamberlain was the Conservative progressive, Lord Randolph Churchill, leader of the party in the Commons and now Chancellor of the Exchequer. However, he pushed faster and farther than Salisbury was willing to go and before Christmas was out of office. The departure of Lord Randolph from the Conservative front bench drove Chamberlain into an exploration of the possibilities for reunion of the Liberal Party – possibilities that eventually proved illusory.

During this exploration, however, working from his study in Highbury, Chamberlain demonstrated his capacity for concrete policy creation to address

Ireland's problems, just as he had a decade earlier for Birmingham. Ireland had long been bedevilled by absentee English landowners who rented small parcels of their property to Irish tenant farmers on minimal terms. Chamberlain devised a scheme to transform these tenant farmers into owners of the land they cultivated without great risk to the British taxpayer. The Conservatives and the Liberals soon embraced his proposal. The Liberal majority following Gladstone, however, insisted that the scheme was inadequate unless accompanied by Home Rule. Conservatives on the other hand, in spite of their tender regard for the rights of property, accepted Chamberlain's scheme because it demonstrated his commitment to maintenance of the union with Ireland. His Irish scheme had the further benefit of building a bridge between Chamberlain and the newly appointed Chief Secretary for Ireland, Arthur Balfour, and his uncle Lord Salisbury.

Nevertheless, the period from spring through autumn of 1887 turned out to be the most perilous stretch of time in Chamberlain's career. Never again would he come so close to failure. He found himself broadly without allies at Westminster, with just a handful of reliable adherents in the House of Commons. Even among the Liberals of Birmingham he was sure only of his own constituency. It was in the country at large that he won the most attention. When he headed for Scotland to carry his appeal as a Radical to crofters cleared out by great landowners to make way for stag hunting, Chamberlain attracted a greater following from the national press than anyone but Salisbury and Gladstone.

Back at home, however, his base came under assault from Gladstonians fighting Unionist Liberals for control of the Birmingham Liberal Association. Chamberlain reasserted his dominance only through a resolution of support from his own constituency association. The ardour of even his closest colleagues in promoting the Civic Gospel dimmed. He struggled against the odds that summer to rekindle the fire that had carried the Civic Gospel to the heights of its achievement when he was mayor.

At summer's end therefore, for the first time since the opening of the house four years earlier, he brought Highbury into play as the place to rally support. This rally accentuated the local confines of his support. It drew together local branches of the

National Radical Union that Chamberlain had put together as the National Union of Liberal Federations fell apart. The three men who addressed the rally represented local constituencies in the House of Commons: Powell Williams for Birmingham South, Chamberlain's brother-in-law William Kenrick for Birmingham North, and Joe himself for West Birmingham. Joe put the best gloss he could on the Conservative government's legislative programme for Ireland, praising the Land Bill as an incomplete yet 'great and generous concession' to the tenants of Ireland. However, he criticised the Coercion Bill that the government had introduced to deal with the spreading lawlessness in Ireland as going too far when it proscribed the Irish Land League, and he declared that he would vote against the government on this point if it were challenged in the House of Commons. His remarks lessened the uneasiness of his supporters over coercion but did not ease his own foreboding. He warned Churchill that 'the game is up unless Providence intervenes to save us'.

Providence intervened, as it usually does, in the oddest of ways. During the negotiations on Irish legislation in the spring and early summer between the Liberal Unionist leaders and the Conservative cabinet, Salisbury learned to appreciate Chamberlain's style of conduct. In private Chamberlain emphasised to his Conservative allies the issues on which he would not agree with them, but in public he gave them stout support. Salisbury marked growing respect for his Radical ally by including him among the few guests invited to meet the Queen when she visited Hatfield, Salisbury's stately home. Speaking afterwards with the Queen, Salisbury described Chamberlain as 'rather advanced in some of his views' but 'an honest man' who 'would serve her well some day'.

The skies soon darkened when three members of a crowd that stormed a police station at Mitchelstown in Ireland were shot and killed. Chamberlain struggled in a meeting with his constituents in Birmingham to shift the political agenda back to Britain's needs closer to home. After the meeting, however, he confessed to Churchill that he did 'not feel absolutely certain of a single seat though I *think* I am safe myself'.

He had just accepted a commission that would take him far from Birmingham but would bring him back with a blessing that would turn Highbury at last into a real home.

Chapter Three
MARY

Highbury stood as a reminder of blighted aspirations when Chamberlain headed away on his new mission. His hopes of leading the Liberal Party were shattered, his band of faithful followers tiny and his home base far from secure. Yet Lord Salisbury discerned in Chamberlain a capacity to shape the political landscape, to 'make the weather', as Winston Churchill later put it. And Salisbury, who was Foreign Secretary as well as Prime Minister, had in his gift an appointment that might enable Chamberlain to find his way out of his awkward situation while helping his country out of a diplomatic embarrassment. Salisbury asked him to take charge of a mission to resolve a dispute between the United States and Britain's neighbouring overseas dominion, Canada, over the rich fishing grounds in the off-shore waters of both countries. And Chamberlain agreed.

Chamberlain found his North American trip politically reassuring and personally gratifying. The political leadership in the United States as it recovered from its Civil War was deeply sympathetic to maintenance of union whether in the US or the UK and was also suspicious of the large Irish minority in the United States who corrupted municipal politics, particularly in New York. These reactions, which Chamberlain discovered upon arrival in New York, ensured him a cordial reception both there and in Washington and reinforced his political stance back in Britain. He also received a warm welcome in Canada and particularly in Toronto which greeted his reaffirmation of their bond to the mother country with enthusiasm. Canada fortified his burgeoning imperialism.

However, the political rewards from his diplomatic mission paled in comparison with the personal. Looking much younger than his fifty years, upon arrival in Washington the dashingly attired British High Commissioner instantly became the hit of the social season. To the astonishment of the staff at the British Embassy, he took to dancing and turned out to be 'an accomplished flirt'. He threw himself into an endless round of dinners and dances.

At one of the first, his eye fell upon the daughter, less than half his age, of the Secretary for War in President Cleveland's cabinet, Mary Endicott. The epitome of a Boston Brahmin, Mary's ancestors had come over on the *Mayflower* and she was also connected to the Morgan firm of international bankers in London.

Chamberlain later claimed that Mary attracted his intellect before she captivated his senses – although his senses were captivated quickly. The woman he saw was erect in posture, full figured, her brow 'high & square for a woman', her face open, 'the eyes wonderfully trusting & truthful, & the mouth firm with a tender curve to the lips'. She was at home in the highest levels of political society. Chamberlain sensed in her 'an immense & hitherto untried capacity of love & devotion. The deeps have hardly been stirred at present, but there lie hidden in them courage, resolution, intensity of purpose & a great power of self-sacrifice.' Like many Victorian men, he found self-sacrifice an alluring characteristic in a woman and believed it to be indispensable in a wife. He found in Mary all the qualities that Highbury, his life at the highest levels of British political society and his family needed.

While the speed with which Chamberlain riveted his attention on Mary raised eyebrows in Washington, that did not disconcert him or distract him from his diplomatic mission. On the contrary his determination to win Mary's hand and to press his diplomatic negotiations to a successful conclusion reinforced each other. When a threat to break off negotiations with the US Secretary of State brought agreement to a prospective resolution, Chamberlain put pressure on Mary 'to end all uncertainty. My work here is rapidly drawing to a close & my public duty will constrain me to return to England as soon as it is completed. … Now, therefore, decide. If you are not afraid & will trust me with your happiness, believe me, I will know how to guard it against all the world.' Such peremptory courting brushed the remaining threads of Mary's resistance away. Once Mary had agreed, Chamberlain exploded with pleasure. 'A lady Palmist here says that my line of luck is the most extraordinary that she had ever seen & I begin to believe it. Hurrah! Hurrah! Hurrah! Hurrah!'

He returned home invigorated by his conquest. 'My youth has come back to me,' he told Mary on his fifty-first birthday. During his absence the Gladstonians had made deep inroads into his political base in Birmingham, but he now reasserted and strengthened his grip. He used his newly created Radical Unionist Association to replace the once formidable Liberal Association, now in Gladstonian hands, as the dominant power in the town. Chamberlain sat at the controls of the political life of his town. There was talk of celebrating his achievement with a torch-led march from the town centre to Highbury. Gradually he overcame the ingrained Liberal loathing for the Tories and created a Unionist alliance with them, though it would never be entirely easy.

Eventually he invited the leading Conservatives of Birmingham to dine at Highbury, where he dazzled them with a sumptuous meal on silver plate placed by liveried servants on a blue silk table cloth crossed like the Union Jack with red and white begonias. The New World had also fuelled Chamberlain's imperialism. He told his constituents that the great reward from his fight over Ireland lay in the evidence it produced 'that the great majority of the British nation are proud of … the glorious and united Empire.'

The one great frustration that Chamberlain had to endure at this otherwise buoyant time was his inability to announce his engagement to Mary during the period from February 1888 when he won her consent until the US Presidential Election in November. There was some concern in Democratic Party circles about the engagement of the daughter of a member of Grover Cleveland's cabinet to the British High Commissioner. However, the underlying reason for the protracted delay was the deep reluctance felt by Secretary Endicott concerning his daughter's departure across the Atlantic.

Depressed but undeterred by William Endicott's foot-dragging, Joseph and Mary engaged in a lengthy correspondence. They wrote among other things about the adjustments needed to prepare Highbury for Mary's takeover from Beatrice as chatelaine. While Mary approached the subject apprehensively, the situation prompted Joseph to give fresh thought to provision for all his children. He told Mary how he would like the three young girls, now attending the same boarding school that had served Beatrice so well (in Wimbledon now rather than Fontainebleau), to have a wing of the house with a sitting room and a spare room for a friend. Beatrice would have her own bedroom/boudoir and sitting room while Austen and Neville would have a separate floor with a study and smoking room.

Chamberlain had to give the news of his engagement to the members of his immediate family individually. Mary worried about how, in particular, his older children would react, for Beatrice was two years older, and Austen one year older, than Mary. But the transition of the chatelaine role proceeded smoothly because Beatrice welcomed her release from those duties. And Austen was delighted at his father's obvious joy in his marriage. Highbury had been a sombre home for all Joseph's children, darkened by his inability to deal with the death of his first wife in giving birth to Austen and still more that of his second wife, upon whom he had grown politically as well as personally reliant. Wrapped up in this second loss, he had fled the country without telling his children of her death, and when he returned he forbade mention of her.

As soon as voting was completed in the presidential election, Chamberlain set sail for Washington. The wedding took place in the presence of President Cleveland (who had failed to win re-election), his cabinet and justices of the Supreme Court. Joe and Mary split their honeymoon between the Virginia countryside and the Italian Riviera. By giving a false date for the end of their journey, they contrived to reach Highbury quietly on Christmas Eve.

Mary's arrival transformed Highbury and brought out the purposes for which the house had been built. It was designed to be a showcase for the new arrival at the summit of British political life, a different kind of leader, an urban industrialist amid the landed gentry and aristocracy who had ruled Britain for the past three hundred years, a leader better in tune with the world's premier industrial economy. By the summer of 1887, before he accepted Salisbury's commission to head to the New World, Chamberlain had not achieved the leadership of a major party – the purpose for which Highbury had been designed. But he had arrived at perhaps an even more influential position as head of a small but pivotal faction that appealed to new forces in the country's popular electorate, a faction that determined which of Britain's main political parties would hold power.

That achievement still left Highbury a grand but austere place without much social animation. Mary, who moved at ease in the highest political circles in the United States, brought her social skills and personal warmth to animate the house without attempting to influence Chamberlain's sense of political direction. She began straightaway on Christmas Eve with the immediate family, all radiating delight at her arrival. Next day the extended family made their introductions, beginning with Joseph's oldest brother Arthur who lived nearby. And on New Year's Day the whole clan assembled for a festive dinner that was to become a much-anticipated annual celebration.

The entire town seemed to welcome the attractive and softening conquest that Joe brought back from the New World. The bride and groom, accompanied by his children, were welcomed at a lavish reception in the Town Hall by what the *Illustrated London News* (19 January 1889) described as the best society of Birmingham. 'The great hall had been transformed into a vast and elegant drawing-room; its walls draped with light blue, dazzling with mirrors, hung with Oriental curtains, and beset with handsome sideboards, on which plate and ornaments were displayed ... the floor spread with a great variety of carpets and rugs ... The fine organ played "Hail Columbia!" in honour of Mrs Chamberlain's great and free country.' And she was presented with a pearl necklace, a diamond star and golden jewellery made in Chamberlain's parliamentary constituency. In Mary's eyes these gifts were outshone by the obvious pride Birmingham took in her husband.

Then to London for the parliamentary year. Mary was duly presented at court to the Queen, and she moved with becoming grace, careful to familiarise herself with the etiquette of her new surroundings. Her only lapse was to wear a glove when she kissed the Queen's hand, but that was overlooked in the pleasure she seemed to generate wherever she went. The pleasure was reciprocal when she accompanied Joe to Hardwick Hall the stately home of Lord Hartington, leader of the preponderant Whig contingent among the Liberal Unionists.

Highbury nevertheless remained the primary base for Joe and Mary in the early years of their marriage. Mary moved carefully to place her imprint on the house without treading on Beatrice's toes. She began with her own boudoir, tinting it delicately with silk and satin curtains, screens and upholstery, lining the bookcase with miniature volumes of American poetry, and introducing a rocking chair from her home in Massachusetts.

Highbury provided the space to establish Mary's social stature in Birmingham. Her first 'At Home' there attracted five hundred guests, their carriages lining the road from the centre of the town to its rural margin. Highbury also gave her husband the space that their London home could not provide to rally his supporters in their thousands. The parliamentary year customarily ended in August; and Chamberlain adopted the practice of inviting his constituents in West Birmingham to a garden party at Highbury where, standing on the terrace, he addressed them on the current political situation. This became a regular event after Mary's arrival, and was reported in detail by the national as well as local press. Talking to his constituents as thoughtful electors, he reached beyond them to a national audience.

But Mary's transformation of Highbury was most apparent to the family. She recognised the fitness of its central Hall for the dances she organised to enliven the social life of her step-children. Even Beatrice, whose guiding interest lay in the serious business of educating poor inner-city children, admitted after the first of these dances that she had never enjoyed herself so much.

Mary also extended the delight that everyone in the family took in gardening and the cultivation of flowers. As a welcome before her arrival at Highbury, Joseph had added a house for Mary's favourite roses to his glasshouses. After arrival Mary developed a rose garden outside the house. All Joseph's children shared his love of gardening and participated actively in it. Austen and Ida also threw themselves into the development of the farm that fed the family and its guests. It was stocked with dairy cattle, sheep, pigs, poultry and hives for honey nourished by fields of wild flowers. Four years after Mary's arrival, Chamberlain more than doubled the acreage of the Highbury estate with the acquisition of bordering land owned by the Cadburys.

He extended the political sway of Highbury along with its acreage. Highbury stood just inside the parliamentary constituency of East Worcestershire. Drawing upon the gratitude of the Conservative leadership for his decisive support for Lord Salisbury's government in the House of Commons, Chamberlain forced the reluctant

Conservative gentry of East Worcestershire to accept his son Austen as the Unionist candidate in the coming general election.

Austen then carried the seat easily. His victory figured in the Unionist sweep in the general election of 1892 over the counties of Staffordshire, Warwickshire and Worcestershire as well as Birmingham, the area that came to be known as Chamberlain's Duchy. They won 30 of the 39 seats in this area, enough to deny Gladstone's Liberals the majority they expected and to ensure that Chamberlain 'made the weather' politically for the rest of the century.

Joseph's political importance had been further enhanced upon his election as Liberal Unionist leader in the House of Commons when Hartington moved up to the House of Lords upon the death of his father, the Duke of Devonshire. Though the conservatively inclined Whigs were predominant in the Liberal Unionist party, they recognised, as did the Conservatives, that Chamberlain and the policies he championed carried decisive weight with the electorate. That weight heightened the prestige of Highbury.

Chamberlain's increased political influence encouraged him to quicken the pace of Unionist policy on social issues. And here again Highbury proved useful. It provided a quiet venue away from the prying eyes of the press to discuss vexed social issues with non-political experts. One of the most contentious issues among the various political parties and religious denominations in Birmingham was regulation of the drink trade. Chamberlain astonished his Nonconformist friends by inviting two bishops of the Established Church to join them along with Teetotallers, Conservatives and Gladstonians to discuss this issue over the dining table at Highbury, followed by frank and good-tempered discussion to find some practicable solution. Chamberlain repeatedly invited Charles Booth, a well-respected writer on social issues, to Highbury for the weekend to canvass ways of providing old age pensions without discouraging thrift or burdening the taxpayer.

Highbury now lived up to all of Chamberlain's desires for the estate, and he never contemplated a move out to the country. Highbury symbolised Chamberlain's brand of politics just as Chatsworth became synonymous with the Duke of Devonshire who had inherited it, and Hatfield became synonymous with Lord Salisbury. The centrality of these figures was accentuated by Gladstone's retirement as leader of the Liberal Party and Prime Minister.

Highbury stood at its peak of influence between the general elections of 1892 and 1895. Without official position in the government, Chamberlain was free to spend weekends there during the parliamentary session rather than in London. Austen's election to the House of Commons increased the intensity of political talk at the family dinner table. The girls joined in with quiet encouragement from Mary who provided a calming influence. And the flow of weekend visits from Joseph's close party colleagues and advisors enriched the conversation. Only Neville was missing, away in the Bahamas tending a major but ultimately disastrous investment made by his father in a sisal plantation. Long letters from Neville passed excitedly from hand to hand at Highbury, but he missed out on immediate involvement. Weekend dining at Highbury was perhaps the liveliest political forum in the kingdom.

Chapter Four
SOUTH AFRICA: THE IMPERIAL TURNING POINT

The fall of the Liberal government in June 1895, its replacement by a coalition Unionist ministry led by Lord Salisbury, and the general election that ensued transformed the function of Highbury. Chamberlain's headquarters moved elsewhere. His acceptance of high office in the new government was bound to keep him in London while Parliament was in session. The post that he asked for as Secretary of State for the Colonies certainly did so.

His weight in national politics was more personal than locational and moved with him. But the character of Highbury changed slowly during his prolonged absences. It became a place of escape from the demands of London. Under Mary's influence it also grew lighter and brighter in décor, and more of a home for the family.

Highbury was nevertheless darkened for the rest of the century by trouble in South Africa which grew eventually all-consuming. In spite of Chamberlain's imperial preoccupations, however, his one enduring achievement from these years arose locally with the founding of the University of Birmingham.

The demands of the 1895 election took him immediately away from Highbury. He was ready for the election. He had seen to the creation of a Midlands Liberal Unionist Association since the last general election in order to improve the performance of the party within his electoral 'Duchy'. Organised from Highbury, the association was grounded in each polling district in Birmingham and extended into every constituency in Worcestershire, Warwickshire and Staffordshire where it increased party membership ten- and sometimes twenty-fold. Chamberlain felt so strong in Birmingham by the time the general election was called that he spent almost the entire campaign in his surrounding Duchy and in a few marginal constituencies elsewhere.

The results provided still more evidence of his electoral pulling power. His Midland organisation improved on the already good Unionist result of 1892. Writing from Highbury, Chamberlain boasted that Unionists had increased their grip on his Duchy from 34 to 38 of its 44 seats. This achievement lost its distinction amid the national tide in which Liberal Unionist representation in the new House of Commons increased by fifty per cent. Their alliance with the Conservatives gave Lord Salisbury's Unionist government an enormous majority, unmatched since the Great Reform Act of 1832.

The demands of the election gave Chamberlain little opportunity to see much of the Colonial Office during the summer months, and left him in almost desperate need of a holiday. He embarked early in September to France and Spain with a visit to Gibraltar, and did not return to England for two months.

He headed then first to Prince's Gardens in London, where he began to fulfil the demands that the Colonial Office made upon him. The approach of Christmas enabled him to return to Highbury in early December. The responsibilities of government modified the guest list for dinner parties there. The Duke of Devonshire, who took charge of education in the new government, stayed at Highbury to speak at the opening of a technical school in Birmingham. Captain Lugard, who was extending British interests in West Africa, added to the small party. The dinner was followed by a huge reception for four hundred to meet the officers of the Unionist Associations of Birmingham, all entertained by a band in the Hall.

Given express communication by post and special carrier, Chamberlain could remain at Highbury in almost instant touch with the Colonial Office in London and with Salisbury at Hatfield. The two men had overlapping concerns to deal with through the holidays. Grover Cleveland, who had returned to the US Presidency, threatened Britain with war over a border dispute between Venezuela and British Guiana. War also threatened to erupt over the border between Bechuanaland, another British colonial possession, and the Transvaal in southern Africa. The Transvaal, over which Britain claimed suzerainty, was peopled mainly by Afrikaner or Boer farmers who resented Britain's claims and the pretensions of an English-speaking, predominantly British minority, known as uitlanders, who owned and ran the rich gold mines of Johannesburg.

Both conflicts approached crisis point between Christmas and the New Year. Chamberlain was initially more concerned to find a resolution to the conflict with the United States. T.F. Bayard, the United States ambassador to Great Britain, had been Secretary of State during Chamberlain's fisheries negotiations in Washington, and was a guest at Highbury after the marriage with Mary. Joe hoped to reach an understanding with him.

But this concern was overtaken by a rapid deterioration of the situation in southern Africa. Joe had been aware for some time that discontent among the British minority in the Transvaal with its Boer government might erupt into rebellion, and he had agreed to the positioning of a small armed force in Bechuanaland, bordering on the Transvaal, to support the rebellion when it occurred. However, after Christmas, just as uitlander discontent in Johannesburg began to subside, the armed force in Bechuanaland led by Captain Jameson decided, without encouragement elsewhere in southern Africa or from Great Britain, to invade the Transvaal anyway.

Like a bolt of lightning, the news struck Chamberlain at Highbury as he prepared for the annual staff Christmas ball. 'If this succeeds it will ruin me,' he told Mary, 'I am going up to London to crush it.' Acting swiftly while taking care not to disrupt the party, he caught the 12.50 am train and reached his empty London house at 4 am on New Year's Eve. Mary managed to telegraph ahead so that a bed and fire would be prepared for him.

Without waiting to find out how Jameson's raid had fared, Chamberlain issued a resolution to the British and southern African press condemning it. Only by doing so could he allay suspicion that Britain had prompted the raid. The response at home and abroad validated his judgement. Liberals at home and in southern Africa congratulated him while Kaiser Wilhelm of Germany highlighted the danger to British interests by praising the Boer government of the Transvaal for resisting the raid, which had quickly collapsed. Chamberlain's action established him as the leading force in imperial politics for the rest of the century.

In the wake of the Jameson Raid, the functions of Highbury changed for all the Chamberlains. Debate in Parliament swirled around the Jameson Raid and its implications for Britain and for Chamberlain personally as Colonial Secretary. It kept him in London, apart from the briefest of returns to Highbury. For several weeks Mary managed only fleeting reunions with her husband and had to rely upon his brothers in Birmingham to host the social engagements to which the family were committed. Austen, in his office as Civil Lord of the Admiralty, was held at Westminster as tightly as his father. Prince's Gardens became his principal residence for the parliamentary session, while his bedroom and smoking room at Highbury were redecorated. The girls did their best to maintain their father's presence at the family's annual New Year gathering by adorning the Hall with photographs of him.

Mary took advantage of her prolonged stay in Highbury to lighten the arrangement of the central Hall. She banished the big ottoman from its centre, shifted the palm tree to the edge and grouped arm chairs and a small sofa to make more room for sitting comfortably and reading – to the delight of the family, though not of Joseph.

Meanwhile his prominence in the political debate across the country further enhanced his standing in Birmingham. When he managed a brief return towards the end of January, he was greeted at the station by enthusiastic supporters, shouting 'Three cheers for Joey' and 'Good for our Joe' into the windows of the carriage that took him home. The Kings Heath fire engine accompanied the carriage to Highbury, causing Joe to wonder for a moment if a fire had broken out there.

Work continued on the house and grounds regardless of his absence in London. Electric wiring had damaged the Drawing Room. Mary used the opportunity to begin redecorating her downstairs room. Quietly abandoning the Gothic décor beloved by the original architect and by Joseph, Mary embraced a lighter Italian renaissance style in keeping with the furniture she had brought from the United States. Outside, the farm and associated buildings were extended.

The demands upon Chamberlain in London were so intense that when he managed an escape to Highbury he slept in late. In February the family established Prince's Gardens as well as Highbury as their home. But Prince's Gardens lacked the gardens and glasshouses in which they all took delight. By Easter both Joseph and Mary were beginning to treat Highbury in effect as their country retreat. They wandered around the grounds and fields, inspecting everything and enjoying its 'spring beauty'. Mary told her mother that she and Joe found 'it very refreshing to be quietly here with no one to disturb the tranquillity of the country'.

They were therefore acutely dismayed as terraced housing sprang up just south of

ELEVATION LOOKING

© Birmingham Museums Trust

Courtesy of Martin Ward and Keeling

Architectural designs for the house, in Venetian Gothic style, by Martin and Chamberlain, 1878.
The Birmingham architectural partnership of John Henry Chamberlain (left) and William Martin (right) was one of the most prominent of the time. John Henry was not related to Joseph Chamberlain but was a close political associate.

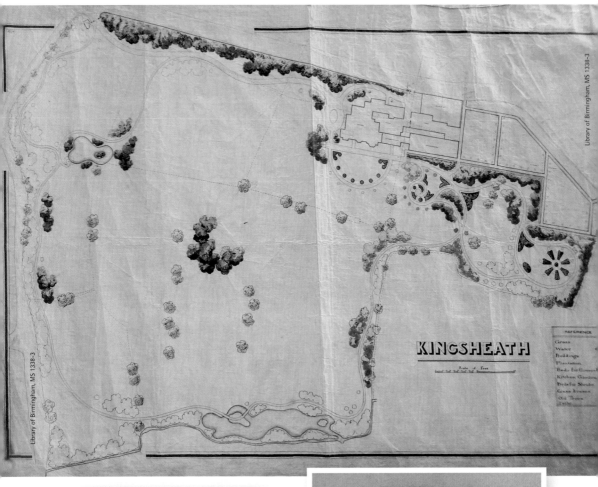

Library of Birmingham, MS 1338-3

KINGSHEATH

Scale of Feet

Library of Birmingham, MS 1338-3

REFERENCE

Grass
Water
Buildings
Plantation
Beds for flowers
Kitchen Garden
Beds for Shrubs
Glass houses
Old Trees
Paths

REFERENCE

Grass
Water
Buildings
Plantation
Beds for flowers
Kitchen Garden
Beds for Shrubs
Glass houses
Old Trees
Paths

Library of Birmingham, MS 1338-3

The Museum of English Rural Life / Landscape Institute [Milner-White & Son Collection]

Design for the landscape of Highbury, 1879, by Edward Milner (bottom right).
Milner was a protégé of Joseph Paxton, the head gardener at Chatsworth and designer of the Crystal Palace.

30

Reproduced with permission of The Library of Birmingham, WK/M6/47

Highbury *c.* 1903, showing the
original driveway.

© Cadbury Research Library: Special Collections

On the east side of the house were the conservatory and a
series of glasshouses, home to Chamberlain's famous orchid
collection. By 1903 there were 25 glasshouses, but most were
demolished in 1922.

© Cadbury Research Library: Special Collections

Maintaining the grounds required a large team of
gardeners, under the control of the head gardener,
who lived on the estate.

"THE CHERUB!"

"THERE'S A SWEET LITTLE CHAMBERLAIN SITS UP ALOFT,
TO KEEP WATCH FOR THE LIFE OF POOR JACK!"

© Mary Evans Picture Library

Chamberlain's favourite *Punch* political cartoon that he kept in the library. Political satire was an integral part of British culture and the family collected many of the cartoons that featured Chamberlain.

The London town house, 40 Prince's Gardens, Knightsbridge, where the family resided for the parliamentary season (second from the right). Highbury was considered the country house, despite being located on the outskirts of Birmingham.

THE HARD-WORKED LEISURE OF AN EX-MINISTER: MR. CHAMBERLAIN IN HIS STUDY ENGAGED ON THE ENORMOUS CORRESPONDENCE INVOLVED BY THE FISCAL CAMPAIGN.

DRAWN BY S. BEGG, OUR SPECIAL ARTIST, DURING A SITTING GRANTED BY MR. CHAMBERLAIN AT HIGHBURY.

Chamberlain orchestrated the tariff reform campaign from the Library at Highbury, assisted by his personal secretary, Mr. Wilson.

© Cadbury Research Library: Special Collections

© Illustrated London News Ltd/Mary Evans

Reproduced with the permission of the Library of Birmingham, Birmingham Faces and Places

Distinguished visitors at Highbury: Lord Camperdown, Mrs Joseph Chamberlain, Duke of St. Albans, Earl Selbourne, Marquis of Hartington, Duchess of St. Albans, Lady Palmer and the Right Hon. Joseph Chamberlain, M.P.
The Marquis of Hartington (later 8th Duke of Devonshire) stayed at Highbury on several occasions until political differences caused a rift.

© Cadbury Research Library: Special Collections

© Illustrated London News Ltd/Mary Evans

Mary Crowninshield Endicott, married Joseph Chamberlain on 15 November 1888 in Washington DC.

Orchids were a personal passion and became a trademark feature of Chamberlain's image. Fresh buttonholes were sent from the Highbury glasshouses to London throughout the season.

Inside the conservatory: Joseph with wife Mary (seated left), eldest son Austen and daughters Beatrice (rear), Ida and Hilda (seated right) and Ethel (front). Neville is missing from the family group, away in the Bahamas.

Family visitors and important guests would often take tea and relax in the landscaped grounds or in one of the more formal gardens.

© Cadbury Research Library: Special Collections

© Cadbury Research Library: Special Collections

Mary Chamberlain preferred less formal arrangements and added couches and chairs in the Hall for house guests to read and write letters in comfort. Everything could be moved for dances or other entertainments.

A personal ambition achieved with the new university buildings and clocktower under construction *c.* 1908. Now affectionately known as 'Old Joe', the commemorative clocktower to the first chancellor still watches over the University of Birmingham today.

© Cadbury Research Library: Special Collections

the estate in Kings Heath, all too visible from Highbury. The relentless march of the builders continued in the following years, spreading out towards the Lickey Hills. Chamberlain felt it so keenly that briefly he considered renting a place in the country. But the rehabilitative powers of gardening and his insistent attachment to Birmingham held him back.

The demands and pace of life in London intensified for Mary as well as Joseph. She was in charge of their social responsibilities to which the Colonial Office added greatly. Birmingham brought extra demands with Joseph required as main speaker at a dinner in honour of the new Lord Mayor. He worked on his speech in the corner of the carriage beside Mary as they made their way to the city.

Meanwhile debate on South Africa continued unabated in the House of Commons, holding Joseph there sometimes through the night. The return of Neville, very thin and worn, with confirmation of the failure of the sisal investment in which Joseph had so heavily invested, added to the family's concerns.

Tired but ultimately unscathed by the debate in the Commons, Joe could not finally escape from London until the middle of August. 'I have been & am still so busy', Mary reported to her mother, 'that until we reach Highbury tomorrow night I shall not really feel that we are free.' Joe then delighted her with news that he had booked passage for them at the end of the month to Massachusetts for three quiet weeks at her family farm. He spent the fortnight before departure happy in his glasshouses and the garden, having tea with Mary in the Dairy and playing bowls on the lawn, one of his rare sporting activities.

No sooner was he back from Massachusetts than Lord Salisbury summoned him to work. At the beginning of December Mary complained that Joe had had only two days at Highbury. At last before Christmas Joe and Austen joined Mary in wandering over the grounds of Highbury and inspecting the trees that they had planted to hide the Kings Heath housing development.

Their time at Highbury was never long enough for Mary. She took delight in the lighter décor of her at last refinished boudoir and the simpler patterning of its carpet. Physically more active than her husband, she took to bicycling, often along with his younger daughters Ida and Hilda, venturing to the furthest southern outskirts of

Birmingham. She was dismayed by the social demands away from Highbury that continued to interrupt their holiday and by the resumption of parliamentary activity that necessitated their return to London in mid-January. She much preferred the spaces of Highbury to 'our limited London quarters' where 'we all seem to be tumbling over each other'.

Though Joseph lived for his work, its demands took a toll on his health, with prolonged colds and bouts of gout. And those demands grew as he set the pace of domestic reform as well as imperial policy in the Unionist government, initiating its most progressive measure, the Employers' Liability Bill for industrial accidents.

The demands of London reached a crescendo in July 1897 with the Diamond Jubilee celebration of Queen Victoria's coronation. 'Parliament is over!' Mary wrote joyfully to her mother at the end of the first week of August. 'When I sleep in my old four-poster tomorrow night & reflect that there are five or six months with no H. of Commons, no S. African Committee, no Rand dregs and the prospect of some free time in the immediate future I shall draw a long breath of relief.' She loved the space of Highbury 'after so many months in a town house with no extra room for anybody'. She rejoiced in the 'cool soft breeze flowing in at the open window,' in contrast to 'that stuffy Morning Room in London – where heat & black & half the dinners of The Mews come in when I open the window & where the atmosphere is heavy & dulling'. Joseph too soon looked better, though he still suffered from neuralgia. They headed off in the middle of the month for a holiday in Switzerland with Joseph's youngest daughter Ethel, sadly showing early signs of what was to prove a fatal disease.

After their Swiss holiday, Mary struggled to ease her husband's working pace. He had a series of major speeches to deliver that autumn. Mary dragged him out of the house in the middle of the day, fearful that otherwise he would remain 'buried in his Library all day & most of the night'.

He carried his appetite for work wherever he went. Highbury enabled him to devote attention to an idea Mary said he had 'had for many years but which now for the first time has come to be "practical politics"'. A new Act of Parliament reorganised the governing body of the local post-secondary institution, Mason College. Chamberlain was now its first President, and he seized the opportunity to make perhaps his most enduring contribution to Birmingham: to transform the college into a university. 'I should die content with my work in Birmingham', he declared in the New Year, 'if I could see a university established.'

Without deflecting his concerns from the city, the New Year further added to his responsibilities and drew international attention to the British statesman from Birmingham. The year began with the seizure by Russia and Germany of ports that opened China up to what had been a predominantly British sphere of influence. By Easter the international situation had been further exacerbated by the outbreak of war between Spain and the United States. These developments precipitated debate within the British cabinet over Lord Salisbury's cautious conduct of foreign policy and Chamberlain's more assertive stance. Although Salisbury was the older of the two by just six years, he was in failing health while Chamberlain stood at the height of his powers. The two men sought to explain their approaches in general terms to their electoral supporters, Salisbury to the Conservative Primrose League, Chamberlain to the annual meeting of the Birmingham Liberal Unionist Association.

It became the first in a series of speeches of international importance that Chamberlain wrote and delivered from his power base. Chamberlain's address to the Birmingham Liberal Unionists, delivered in the Town Hall in mid-May, recalled to his eldest sister Mary the spell-binding speeches she had heard there in her youth from the great Radical orator John Bright. Chamberlain's speech was particularly moving for his wife because she had a part in its formation, relaying news from the United States on its war with Spain.

The encroachment of Russia and Germany on the British market in China prompted Chamberlain to look for allies to strengthen Britain's hand. He found the most congenial ally in the United States which shared a common political culture with Britain and wanted, like Britain, to keep the Chinese market open for international commerce without fear or favour. But while the United States was preoccupied with its war with Spain, Chamberlain sought a more immediately useful understanding with Germany.

His search for closer relations with Germany divided the British cabinet, undercutting Salisbury's control of foreign policy without winning a cordial response from Germany. The response from the United States, while purely sentimental, was more heartening. The *New York Times* hailed Chamberlain's address as the 'most memorable speech that an English audience in either hemisphere has listened to in a generation'.

He could not get away from London until mid-August when he surprised and delighted Mary with the news that he had booked another passage for them from Liverpool to the Endicott family farm in Massachusetts at the end of the month.

Two months later Mary was back in Highbury ensconced in the Library opposite Joseph while he worked away at official papers. His main concern for the rest of the year was the string of speeches he had agreed to give around the country, often focused on foreign and imperial affairs. Mary observed him '… struggling with speeches for Manchester. At first in the depths – nothing to say – then he got started – now he has too much & has to cut it down – So go the familiar stages.' Back at Highbury, he continued work on the projected University of Birmingham, bringing its leaders together with colleagues from the Colonial Office who were preoccupied by the situation in South Africa.

Christmas 1898 was a special one for the Chamberlains, the first time since Joseph's marriage to Mary that the whole family would be together. They all threw themselves into the celebrations, and it proved to be their happiest. A great tree was positioned at the window end of the Dining Room with just enough room to walk around, its top brushing the ceiling. Joe's daughters and Mary spent hours decorating it with balls, beads, tinsel stars and 'glassicles', cotton wool to represent snow and 90 candles for illumination. Joseph's multitude of nieces and nephews arrived early in the afternoon, played games until 5 and then had tea in the breakfast room followed by darkened lights in the great Hall where Beatrice told them a story about Father Christmas. This was interrupted by a knock on the door, and in walked 'Father Christmas'. Neville was padded with three down cushions and three Shetland shawls, his outfit decorated with holly, and his pockets stuffed with toys. So effectively was he disguised that little Evelyn Nettlefold exclaimed: 'Oh, isn't it kind of Father Christmas to come to the party!'

The children followed 'Father Christmas' up the stairs, round the gallery and back down into the Dining Room. They gasped at the tree with all its illuminations and then made a circle round it. 'Father Christmas' gave each of them a present and allowed them to choose what they wanted off the tree. Joseph suggested that those with musical instruments should march round the Hall, and seven trumpets, five drums and other instruments joined in a noisy procession. After a further game they formed another line, starting with the youngest, and processed past Joseph. He presented each of them with a purse, a new half-crown for the little ones and a five-shilling piece for the older children.

Highbury remained a relaxing refuge for the Chamberlains as the century drew to a close, until South Africa again intruded on its peace as it had over Christmas in 1895. The demands of the Colonial Office held Joseph captive in London through Easter 1899 at repeated cost to his health, neuralgia being punctuated by influenza and gout. Highbury offered him otherwise his only outdoor exercise, lawn bowling with Mary. She revelled in the springtime sun, filling the garden with daffodils, crocuses and primroses after the 'pea-souper' fogs and 'poisonous air' of London. Highbury also enabled Joseph to push ahead with his search for competitive match funding for the University of Birmingham from Andrew Carnegie and Lord Strathcona.

By June, however, the conflicting pressures from South Africa between the South African Republic led by President Kruger and the mining interests of Johannesburg championed by the British High Commissioner in Cape Town, Sir Alfred Milner, threatened to erupt in war. While Chamberlain sought recognition of Britain as the paramount power in South Africa, he recognised that there was little appetite in Britain for war.

He therefore returned to his political base to define the British position on the conflict in terms that he hoped the country would endorse. Speaking to the Liberal Unionist Association of Birmingham, he argued that Kruger's regime was 'not only oppressive and unjust' but constituted 'a menace to British interests and a serious danger to our position as the paramount Power in South Africa'. In doing so, he raised the stakes in the controversy. However, to Milner's dismay, he was not yet ready to confront Kruger with an ultimatum. Chamberlain ended his speech instead by appealing to 'our loyal Dutch subjects in Cape Colony' to persuade Kruger 'to make the necessary concessions', particularly in ceding some political power to the uitlanders of Johannesburg.

The press in Britain responded well to this presentation, and there were encouraging as well as disturbing developments in southern Africa. The Chamberlains returned hopefully to Highbury at the close of the parliamentary year in August. Joe looked forward to a project in the grounds of the house suggested by Hilda for a 'Pleasance', enclosing a small field inside a beech hedge with a pleasure garden at one end and an informal garden at the other. He sat up late completing the plans for the planting of this 'Pleasance' and talked wistfully of giving up politics to become a market gardener.

Then, after barely a week of holiday, he was summoned back to London. Mary reacted 'very full of vengeance & not at all imbued with Christian charity towards Kruger'. When pressed, Kruger backed away from assurances of enlarged political representation of the Johannesburg uitlanders. Joe returned to Birmingham, resolved to rally public support for a stiffened British response to Kruger. Using the occasion of a garden party at Highbury, he described how Kruger 'dribbles out reforms like water from a squeezed sponge' and warned that if he procrastinated much longer, Britain would widen its demands in order to secure 'conditions which once for all shall establish which is the paramount Power in South Africa'.

His speech from the terrace at Highbury produced a sharply divided response in Britain between those who thought it too aggressive and those who thought it inadequately resolute. However, when Kruger backed away from his most recent concessions and reverted to a hard line on enfranchising uitlanders, opinion in Britain swung behind Chamberlain. Though he recognised that a large minority continued to resist the dominant trend, he was confident that the British now understood that a greater issue than uitlander grievances was at stake, that not only the supremacy of Great Britain in South Africa but its 'existence as a great Power in the world are involved in the result of our present controversy'. He now possessed the general support at home which he would need in the event of war or – and he had not quite lost hope – if he were to induce Kruger to back down.

Chapter Five
WAR

This speech made Highbury more than ever the house where the political weather was made, and confirmed Chamberlain's centrality in British and imperial politics. However, the war to which his speech led damaged his brand of imperialism irretrievably. The war overstretched Britain's military and financial capacity and the appetite of the country for further ventures of this sort. Chamberlain again became the most divisive figure in British politics as he had been in the fight over Irish Home Rule.

The coming of the Boer War also tied Joseph and Mary closer than ever to Highbury. They could not leave for their usual summer holiday abroad while Britain and Kruger's republic were publishing their final statements and preparing for hostilities. Prolonged residence at home made Joe and Mary more sensitive to its pleasures and shortcomings. They continued ever more elaborate developments of their 'Pleasance' and relished the beauty of their maturing gardens. At the same time their dismay also deepened over the industrial chimneys and 'rows and rows of slate roofs' being built between Highbury and their view of the Lickey Hills. Mary felt Highbury 'much injured' but refrained from mentioning it to Joseph in view of his obvious distress.

He had to be ready to leave for London at a moment's notice. Meanwhile telegrams poured in day and night, sometimes pulling him out of bed through the early hours of the morning. They took a toll on his health. Nevertheless, he secured overwhelming support at home once Kruger abandoned any interest in a peaceful settlement and opted for defiance.

War duly began before the end of October but the early encounters proved disastrous for the British. They immediately lost two regiments to the Boers who were fighting on home ground against a distant power that had grossly underestimated its opponent. And things rapidly deteriorated with the defeat of three major British forces in 'Black Week' early in December.

'Black Week' shattered Chamberlain's political agenda for Britain and its empire. The scene at Highbury had already changed with the early advent of winter. It turned the ponds into skating rinks and stripped the trees back to what Mary described as their 'native ugliness', unable to hide the houses of Kings Heath. Briefly, Joseph felt broken in spirit. He had to struggle for words even on his home turf when he distributed prizes at the Municipal School of Art. 'The next few weeks must be a very anxious time', he wrote to Mary's mother on Christmas Eve: 'They will show whether we can relieve the beleaguered garrisons & to what extent the rebellion will spread in Cape Colony, but', he continued, regaining his strength of purpose, 'whether we are successful or whether we have to face further sacrifices I do not doubt the result in the end.'

The floundering war effort affected everyone in the family. The lists of British dead and wounded 'contain names we know', Mary lamented, '& there is not the comfort of feeling that any real progress in the war has been made'. Ida took charge of distributing financial support to families near Highbury where the breadwinner had joined the armed forces in South Africa. Mary reported that as 'far as Ida knows, no husbands have been reported killed or wounded', but one day she might have to be the bearer of bad news. By the end of the year Mary, Ida, Hilda and the servants at Highbury were knitting caps and socks for the troops, and they organised further production in neighbouring households. In contrast, the business that Neville had taken charge of, Hoskins and Sons, stood to benefit from the war. Hoskins produced ships berths which were rapidly adapted for use in field hospitals, ultimately exposing the family to accusations of war profiteering.

The opening of the new century drew attention away from Highbury to the debate that the war precipitated in Parliament. The survival of the government was now in some doubt. More than ever, Joseph stood at the epicentre of the debate. Mary settled into Prince's Gardens to observe from the Ladies' Gallery in the House of Commons. Ida and Hilda remained at Highbury, eventually sending fourteen cases of socks and caps to the troops.

Joe and Mary could not return to Highbury until Easter. Their focus then was on the prospective engagement of Joseph's youngest daughter Ethel, in spite of her precarious health, to Whitmore Lionel (Lio) Richards, a friend of Neville from their schooldays at Rugby. Flu sent Joseph to bed during the holiday, but Mary arranged a bicycle trip to Broadway in the Cotswolds. 'Somehow Ida, Hilda, Neville and I were together most of the time', she reported, in hopes that Lio would make good use of his time with Ethel. He did indeed; their engagement was announced two weeks later.

On the day of the announcement Mary received word of the death of her father. This sad but not unexpected news made Highbury more important for her than ever. She implored her mother to come to her there – because the demands on Joseph in Britain prevented Mary from joining her mother in Massachusetts.

The mood in Britain had changed in March with its first military success in the relief of Ladysmith. By May Britain stood on the verge of what looked like decisive victory. That prospect brought Joseph back from London to Birmingham where he often issued key statements of British policy, in this case the government's terms for peace. But far from freeing him for a summer holiday in Massachusetts, his involvement in British politics only deepened.

Mrs Endicott had promptly agreed to her daughter's request to visit. Mary and Neville welcomed her at Liverpool in the middle of June, and she settled straightaway at Highbury. Mary stayed with her there for the remainder of the summer while the rest of the family continued their routine of weeks in London and weekends at Highbury. They returned there at the end of the parliamentary year in August for the wedding of Ethel and Lio at the Unitarian Church of the Messiah in the centre of Birmingham. Mary and Mrs Endicott then set off for two months of sightseeing on the Continent.

They left Joseph at Highbury absorbed in a campaign to turn the apparent outcome of the war into a vindication of his imperialism. As usual he accelerated the political pace by securing an early dissolution of Parliament and a fresh general election. The British forces in South Africa pushed relentlessly towards an annexation of the Transvaal which their new commander-in-chief, Lord Roberts, secured on 1 September. There were already indications of the need for caution with the first signs of guerrilla warfare in August. But Chamberlain wanted a fresh electoral mandate before any Liberal revival in Britain could encourage Kruger's hope for the continued autonomy of the South African Republic.

Chamberlain secured what he sought. The combined forces of Conservatives and Liberal Unionists retained their majority at the dissolution, breaking the electoral norm of recent years when the major British parties had alternated in power. Joe set the pattern for regional contests in this general election by conducting his campaign from Highbury, and confining it almost entirely to the West Midlands. The strategy worked, although he was disappointed that the Unionist contingent fared no better than in 1895.

The Liberals were demoralised by internal divisions between Liberal Imperialists who supported the war, Little Englanders who opposed it, and those like the party leader Sir Henry Campbell-Bannerman who were chiefly concerned to hold the Party together. However, the most ardent spirits among them, led by the aspiring Welshman David Lloyd George, sought to compensate for their enfeebling divisions by attacking the Chamberlain family personally for war profiteering. This attack, launched before the general election and intensified afterwards, focused primarily on Joe's closest brother, Arthur. Arthur was essentially a businessman in search of profit for his company, Kynochs, which manufactured the basic military explosive, cordite. The part that cordite could play in politics was evident back in 1895 when it helped to bring down the Liberal government because supplies were inadequate. There was nothing anomalous about that for the Birmingham economy, in which the manufacture of armaments large and small was a prominent feature.

However, it left Arthur vulnerable to Lloyd George's smears on his integrity – smears that no responsible statesman had yet thought to place on the integrity of the landed gentry and aristocracy who used their parliamentary might to defend their agricultural interests. Joseph felt hurt as never before by the attack on the integrity of Arthur, who was also the neighbour closest to Highbury. 'My relations are all men of business,' Joseph told the House of Commons. 'I come of a family which boasts nothing of distinguished birth, or of inherited wealth; but who have a record – an unbroken record of nearly two centuries – of unstained commercial integrity and honour. … an attack upon that affects me more than any other attack that could be made.' He never forgot or forgave the members of the Liberal opposition who voted in favour of Lloyd George's censure motion.

The Chamberlains found themselves in the New Year split between their two houses. While Highbury remained their primary home, the seemingly irrepressible guerrilla war that continued in South Africa fuelled bitter parliamentary debate that kept them in Prince's Gardens, apart from during the Easter and Whitsun holidays into August. Then the continuing debate in the press on the situation in South Africa imprisoned them in Highbury for the rest of the year, denying Joe and Mary the Caribbean holiday that Mary in particular longed for.

Their lives had been brightened by the birth in June of a granddaughter, Hilda Mary, to Ethel and Lio at their home in London. The baby flourished, but Ethel was slow to recover. The consequences of childbirth were not the problem. Ethel was suffering from what Mary tried to play down as 'her little ailment'. The family avoided the word tuberculosis for another year, encouraged by Ethel's ability to rally under Mary's attentive ministrations. Both Ethel and Hilda Mary required separate nursing that kept them at Highbury over Christmas – to the delight of everyone except for Lio, not least Joseph. Grandfather and granddaughter were much taken with each other. Mary reported happily on a day when Hilda Mary carried on a conversation of coos with Joseph 'which entertained the whole family – so you see the baby worship is in full swing'. Mary dreaded the prospect in the New Year of Ethel and Hilda Mary's departure for their home in London.

Baby worship helped Joseph's anxieties through this year of political paralysis. He found his most constructive work locally with the University of Birmingham. Many of the dinner parties at Highbury during parliamentary vacations brought together the administrative leaders, professors and financial supporters of the university. Robed as chancellor, Joseph presided over its first degree-giving ceremony.

However, it was only in Birmingham that his efforts were crowned with success. The widespread guerrilla warfare in South Africa heartened the Boers of the Transvaal, increasing their support from the large Dutch community in the Cape Colony, heaping scorn upon Britain from Continental European states, weakening the Liberal Imperialists at home who had backed the war, and disheartening the Unionists after their triumph in the recent general election. The impact of the war on the financial position of the government was paradoxical. As long as British forces were engaged in battle, they were assured of financial support from the Exchequer. However, the continuing costs of the war exacerbated the financial dilemma facing the government of mounting costs on all sides exceeding current revenue. Demand was increasing rapidly on domestic issues, particularly in education, as well as for the armed forces whose inadequacy was exposed by the Boer War.

This dilemma would have to be addressed once the war came to an end. It would then raise uncomfortable questions about Chamberlain's priorities. His absorption in imperial concerns had detached him from concerns on his doorstep aside from the new university. That was his only activity in the field of education that did not provoke religious controversy. The crucial question otherwise was how to fund improvement in elementary education and extend provision to the secondary level when most schools were affiliated to the Church of England – and these were the schools that found it hardest to meet the rising standards demanded by the education ministry. The answer taking shape at the ministry was to shift the source of governmental financial support from the municipal to the county level where denominational loyalties were more diffuse. Although not in Birmingham. There Nonconformists remained angry at the privileged position of the Established Church. Chamberlain had given voice to that anger in the 1870s. However, support for the Church of England coursed strongly through the veins of Conservatives elsewhere in the country upon whom the Unionist alliance now depended.

Another issue even closer to home was a source of painful concern for Chamberlain. Restriction of the alcoholic drinks trade and hence of drunkenness among the labour force was a cause dear to Radical hearts and one for which he had sought a municipal solution in the 1870s. His brother Arthur later moved on to a much tougher stance as chairman of the Birmingham magistrates. By the end of the century Arthur was urging the magistrates to compel brewers to surrender many of their public house licences. Joseph sought a financial compromise, offering the brewers partial compensation for these closures. However, the rationale he offered for his proposal revealed that he had come to share the doubts of his Conservative allies about the effectiveness of governmental regulation in this field. Arthur took offence, and he fell out of sympathy with the general political direction that Joseph was taking. Their estrangement was exposed in February 1902 when Arthur refused to attend the celebration that the City of London staged in Joseph's honour at the Guildhall.

Every other member of the Chamberlain family was on hand to watch Joseph cheered through the city streets – with the foreboding exception of Ethel. She had fallen seriously ill at her home not far from the festivities and was besieged by doctors in search of an explanation. While everyone shied away from calling it tuberculosis, the doctors concluded that only an operation could cure her disease. She was moved into a nursing home for constant care away from her baby daughter, who was placed in Mary's custody. The family took turns during their Easter holiday at Highbury to ensure that one of them visited Ethel in her London nursing home every day. Ethel remained there until the middle of April.

The British forces were doing so well in South Africa a month later that Joseph returned to Highbury to outline his thoughts on a post-war settlement to the Liberal Unionists of Birmingham. He was buoyed up less by the long-delayed prospect of victory than by the outpouring of military support that Britain had received during the war from the white dominions, New Zealand, Australia and Canada – 30,000 troops in all. Chamberlain sought strength from this overseas empire to meet the stiffening economic challenge that Britain faced closer to home. Large continental states such as Germany and the US sought access to the market in Britain which had torn down its defences in embracing free trade. Chamberlain warned his Birmingham audience: 'If we do not take every chance in our power to keep British trade in British hands … we shall deserve the disasters which will infallibly come upon us.'

This challenge to the economic policy which Britain had espoused for the past half-century failed to stimulate the debate that Chamberlain sought. It was overshadowed by the return of Boer negotiators to talks aimed at ending the war. The Treaty of Vereeniging was signed at the end of May. Although Chamberlain described the treaty as 'terms of surrender', it was not as tough as he would have liked. It brought the armed conflict to an end but served to prolong debate about its deeper implications.

Those implications and other consequences of the end of the war diverted Joe's attention from the local base of his power and carried him far from Highbury for a crucial few months at the turn of the year. Lord Salisbury retired as prime minister soon after the war's end and was replaced by the leader of the Conservative party in the House of Commons, Arthur Balfour. Chamberlain readily accepted Balfour's elevation but this weakened Joe's local power base. Balfour sponsored an Education Bill that proposed to give aid from local taxation to enable denominational, largely Church of England schools to meet the rising standards demanded by the education ministry. Balfour's motion met the country's educational need but was anathema to the Nonconformists who were dominant among the Liberal Unionists of Birmingham.

Balfour's elevation also prompted Chamberlain to make more of the stature he had acquired during the war as first minister of the British Empire. He convened a conference of the premiers of the self-governing colonies in connection with the coronation of the new monarch, Edward VII. This conference provided Chamberlain with a golden opportunity to promote the goal he had laid out to his Birmingham constituents for consolidation of the empire through a network of preferential tariffs.

The Canadian premier Laurier embraced this initiative as a way for Britain to respond to the preferential tariff he had already given Britain to favour imports of Canadian wheat. However, Canada did not want its policy of imperial preference to extend to its nascent manufacturing industries. Chamberlain and Laurier shaped their tariff policies to suit the conflicting interests of their two countries. They hoped to find agreement through preferential modification of the modest registration duty that Britain had recently imposed on imported wheat to defray the costs of the Boer War. Although Chamberlain explored this possibility, he failed to secure cabinet agreement to it in the autumn before he set sail on a voyage of imperial reconciliation to South Africa.

His voyage caught the popular imagination abroad but nowhere was this more evident than at home. And it brought Highbury to its pinnacle of fame. With bipartisan cooperation, Birmingham planned to give Chamberlain a farewell to dwarf all previous celebrations in his honour. Following a banquet in the Town Hall, the most remarkable feature of this celebration occurred when Chamberlain left the Town Hall that night for the ride home to Highbury. He was met by a 'sea of fire-lit faces'. Four thousand men from the local artillery, naval reserve, yeomanry and university student body lined the streets leading to Highbury carrying torches. As Chamberlain's carriage moved along, 'the cheering broke into a deep-tongued roar'. The torch-bearers swung in behind, eight abreast, creating a river of flame. Never had Highbury attracted such spectacular attention.

However, when Chamberlain sailed away from Britain's shores next day, he left his power base behind. He expected to return from South Africa next spring in time for the cabinet to agree upon the budget for the New Year, including the registration duty on corn. On the eve of his departure from South Africa, however, Austen warned him that C.T. Richie, recently appointed Chancellor of the Exchequer, threatened to resign if the registration duty on corn was amended preferentially as Chamberlain and the Canadians desired.

Chamberlain sailed home sobered. As so often, his health mirrored his mood, and he came down with gout. Nevertheless, the reception he received on returning to England was everything he could have hoped for. As always, Birmingham stood out in the warmth of his reception. A deputation from the city sent to meet him at Southampton dashed onto the medical tugboat that inspected his ship before it reached port. The cabinet turned out in force to meet the train that carried him to London. Crowds gathered along his route to Prince's Gardens. And the King asked him to report on his mission to South Africa next day. Chamberlain headed straight from the King to see how Ethel was recovering at her convalescence home in Eastbourne, and was relieved to find her looking well.

At last home after five months away, he returned to Highbury, eager to see his glasshouses and orchids. Mary and he were delighted by the 'Dutch garden' developed in their absence, with daffodils in the lower section, tulips in the middle, and irises above. Ethel, Lio and Hilda Mary soon joined them. And by Easter Hilda Mary, whom they called the Cherub, 'had the entire family under her thumb'.

Chamberlain pressed on with his next local initiative, to give Birmingham its own diocese and bishop. This move had little to do with religion but reflected his sense of what befitted a great city. Otherwise, as far as the backlog of business from the Colonial Office would allow, he devoted himself to his orchids. When he returned to London after Easter at Highbury, the family could see a 'difference of tone of his mind … much more inclined to take a vigorous view of things & with a return of what Mary called his "old habit of ideas"'.

By contrast, Mary found everyone low in spirits, from Balfour on down, sensing the unpopularity of the government. The cost to Chamberlain of prolonged absence from his power base became painfully apparent. Had he been on the spot, he could have worn down Richie's opposition or won commanding cabinet support for preferential amendment of the corn duty. Chamberlain had hoped that this modest step would give the government a revitalised sense of imperial purpose. But now Richie's stiffened refusal forced Chamberlain to propose imperial preference in a sweeping and much more contentious form.

He returned to his home base in Birmingham to do so. The city had neutralised Nonconformist opposition to the new Education Act by placing responsibility for local tax support for schools in Nonconformist rather than church-friendly hands – though only in Birmingham. The Liberal Unionists of Birmingham also encouraged Chamberlain to press on with imperial preference. William Ashley, the economist Chamberlain placed in charge of the commerce faculty at the University of Birmingham, undertook to write a book on tariff reform.

So it was to the Liberal Unionists of Birmingham that in May 1903 Chamberlain delivered his plea for imperial preference. Expanding on the precedent Canada had set, he called for 'a treaty of preference and reciprocity with our own children'. He extended his policy to foreign competition by calling for retaliatory tariffs 'whenever our own interests or our relations between our Colonies and ourselves are threatened by other people', particularly the Germans. He invested his appeal with a sense of urgency. 'You have an opportunity', he told his audience, '… you will never have it again.' He turned his appeal in conclusion into a challenging question, asking: 'Whether the people of this country really have it in their hearts to do all that is necessary, even if it occasionally goes against their own prejudices, to consolidate an Empire which can only be maintained by relations of interest as well as by relations of sentiment?'

With that question he set the political agenda for Britain for the remaining lifetime of that parliament. At the same time he reversed the fortunes of both the major parties in a way that he found deeply disconcerting.

Chapter Six
DISRUPTIVE HOMECOMING

Chamberlain's springtime appeal in 1903 for imperial preference transferred his headquarters back home to Birmingham that autumn on an enduring basis. However, his attempt to consolidate the empire through tariffs also had a paradoxically divisive effect. Instead of giving the Unionists a rejuvenating sense of purpose, it split them in three. And although Chamberlain's tariff reformers emerged as the strongest faction of the three, his return to his political base in Birmingham exposed the individuality, indeed the uniqueness, of its regional economy. Birmingham provided a false impression of Britain as a whole, a deception that Chamberlain never recognised.

The immediate impact of his springtime initiative was to plunge the cabinet into internal debate which kept him in London until Parliament rose for its summer recess. The contingent of determined free traders in the cabinet numbered only three but with a potentially dangerous fourth in the Duke of Devonshire. Staunch support for Chamberlain was not much larger. Most of the cabinet sympathised to some extent with the desire of Balfour as prime minister to hold the party together. However, Balfour recognised that the government could not survive without some cooperation from Chamberlain, the strong man in the ministry with the broadest appeal among the electorate.

Towards the end of the summer the two men began to consider an extraordinary relationship in which each of them would work independently where he was most effective: Balfour in the business of government, freeing Chamberlain to convince the country at large to embrace imperial preference. Accordingly, in September Chamberlain left the government on amicable but ill-defined terms and returned to Highbury to launch his nationwide campaign.

The Library at Highbury became his working headquarters – something it had not been since he entered the cabinet in 1895. His Library was nothing like as well staffed as the Colonial Office; consequently, Chamberlain and his single private secretary were soon overwhelmed with letters that ran into their hundreds daily, with frequent visitors coming to consult him directly. Still, he was free from the flow of governmental red boxes which had held him captive in London. He holed himself up in the Library for three weeks to concentrate on the speeches he planned to deliver around the country before the end of the year.

The return to Highbury had a disruptive effect on his family. Chamberlain's resignation, along with the departure of the three insistent free traders and then also of the Duke of Devonshire, necessitated a reconstruction of the cabinet. Crucial in Chamberlain's eyes was the replacement of Ritchie as Chancellor of the Exchequer by Austen. This elevation kept Austen away from Highbury and in London for much of the remainder of the year. And in the New Year he had to set up home away from Highbury in his official residence at 11 Downing Street.

Everyone in the family felt that wrench, especially Austen. However, it was a blow also for Mary, cut off from the soulmate she had found in Austen. Almost identical in age, Austen and Mary were conservative by inclination, unlike Joseph who was restlessly challenging. With Austen away in London, Neville assumed new responsibilities, giving a lead in the tariff reform movement in Birmingham and the West Midlands and keeping a close eye on local elections. Joseph's daughters headed away for holidays on their own. This meant that Highbury lost a good part of its social life, which Mary had done so much to enliven. With Joe hard at work in the Library, Mary compared the two of them sadly to Darby and Joan, the proverbial married couple who led a placid, uneventful life.

For Joseph the next three months were anything but uneventful. His old foe – gout returned under the strain of preparing almost single-handedly for the campaign of speeches that then radiated out from Highbury. Almost single-handedly but not quite because Mary accompanied him to each destination.

There had been nothing quite like this campaign before. The crusade that converted Britain to free trade in the middle of the nineteenth century had been a team effort; and Gladstone's Midlothian campaigns were diffuse in focus.

Without broadening his objective, Chamberlain modified it to what was called tariff reform, embracing retaliatory and some protective tariffs along with imperial preference. He also arrogated some of the functions of government by appointing leading businessmen to an enquiry, rather like a royal commission, on how the tariffs he advocated could be tailored to meet the needs of the differing sectors of the national economy.

His autumn campaign reached its high point appropriately in the largest public arena in Birmingham, Bingley Hall. The preference that Canada offered on wheat from the prairies forced Chamberlain to call for a tariff on foreign wheat, returning to the dreaded Corn Laws. Would that not raise the price of the working man's bread? Free traders made the point graphically in a poster displaying the big and little loaf. Here lay the most persuasive challenge to tariff reform.

To meet it dramatically, Chamberlain commissioned the baking of two loaves to reflect the imperceptible loss in size that his tariff on foreign wheat would bring about. Nervously, his closest adviser remarked, 'you are the only man who could' pull the stunt off, 'and only in Birmingham'. When Chamberlain held up his two loaves in Bingley Hall, 'Birmingham understood & roared and shrieked with delight & called again for the loaves to be held aloft'. 'I think', Mary added, 'that will kill that poster of the big & little loaf in B'ham at all events'.

In January the campaign came to an ambivalent end, however, in the City of London where financial interests differed sufficiently from those of the manufacturing West Midlands to mute its response to Chamberlain's message. On top of this, his solitary campaigning aggravated its toll on his health. He suffered an attack of gout severe enough to send him to his doctors. They discovered strain to his heart and warned him to take a complete holiday soon, if possible for four months.

Barely a week later Powell Williams, the Birmingham MP who was Chamberlain's chief party organiser, buckled under the demands Joe had placed upon him. They had extended beyond the national Liberal Unionist Association and the newly formed Tariff Reform League to include negotiations with the Duke of Devonshire and mobilising support in the House of Commons. It was in the Commons that Powell Williams suddenly had an apoplectic stroke and died the next day. Chamberlain was shattered by the loss and the sense of his own guilt. 'It was my fault,' he told Williams' wife, 'I have worked him to death.' Mary could not imagine how Joe would do without him.

She nevertheless reinforced the doctors' insistence that he leave immediately on holiday. They embarked for Egypt, leaving Neville in charge at Highbury with increasing responsibilities. Highbury acted as a power source among the Chamberlains: absence from Highbury was weakening, presence at Highbury was empowering. Joseph was uneasy about leaving. 11 Downing Street, not Highbury, was now home for Austen, and Austen's consequent loss in power proved enduring. Joseph thought that Austen's appointment as Chancellor would anchor tariff reform in the cabinet. Instead it neutralised Austen.

After barely a month away, Joseph headed home, but too soon. He caught a cold before departure from Cairo. However, his mind was on the deteriorating political situation at home which he sought to survey in letters to his sons. He began with Austen in London but the realisation was dawning that, as Chancellor, Austen was beholden to Balfour as well as to his father.

Joseph therefore turned to Neville at Highbury and commissioned him to replace Powell Williams as organiser of the tariff reform forces in Birmingham and the West Midlands. The threefold division of the Unionists under Balfour's dispiriting leadership turned Chamberlain's attention away from the House of Commons to the party organisation throughout the country where ardent spirits gravitated towards tariff reform. Disregarding his continuing fatigue, Joseph placed Williams' work at the national level on his own shoulders. Back at Highbury by Easter, he brought both his sons and experts led by Ashley from the University of Birmingham together in council. The springtime chill and showers of Highbury did nothing, however, for his health; and for recreation he had to desert the gardens for the glasshouses.

The diminishing prospects for tariff reform nationally enhanced the significance of Highbury for Joe both politically and for recreation. His Liberal Unionists hung on to Powell Williams' seat in the House of Commons, a rare bye-election success in those days when a strongly tariff-reforming Unionist candidate on the outskirts of Chamberlain's electoral Duchy in Shropshire fell to the Liberals. He also lost the assistance of Neville, who departed for Burma to seek consolation for an unhappy romance. But Joseph could always find solace in the glasshouses and gardens in which he continued to develop new features. Visits from Hilda Mary to Highbury were also prolonged to release Ethel whose illness, now unmistakeably tuberculosis, intensified. She travelled to a specialist clinic at Adelboden in Switzerland, leaving Hilda Mary to accompany her grandfather hand-in-hand to the glasshouses.

In his Library he wrote the speeches that he delivered across the country that summer and autumn. More than ever, Highbury served as his headquarters. From Highbury he directed the takeover by tariff reformers of the party organisation, not only of his Liberal Unionists but also of Balfour's Conservatives. When Joe tried to put off requests for meetings from important people by warning that he would not be in London, they made a pilgrimage instead to Highbury. And it was there that his inner circle of counsellors gathered with increasing frequency. The year ended with mixed fortunes: Hilda Mary was thrilled to find a stocking full of little toys on her bed at Highbury while Lio hesitated over the puzzling ups and downs in Ethel's health to find the best time to visit her.

Her condition worsened precipitously in the New Year. Hilda rushed to Adelboden in mid-January and arrived just in time to be at Ethel's bedside when she died. The telegram with this news reached Highbury early in the morning, turning it into a 'house of mourning'. The family struggled to deal with the tragedy. They held a service in the Library at the hour Ethel was laid to rest in the cemetery nestling among the mountains of Adelboden. Joseph led the service, and though he found it hard to speak about Ethel, he did not shut himself up as he had over previous family tragedies. The family walked together afterwards in the garden, sharing their feelings. Still they reeled over the loss, first particularly Ida, then Hilda when she returned, brave but exhausted. Neville returned home, devastated at having been absent when his sister died.

Trying to help everyone else, Mary was eventually struck down with flu that turned into neuritis so serious that she required seaside convalescence. She struggled to understand Lio's need to take Hilda Mary back with him to their home in London and felt that all the joy had left Highbury. Mrs Endicott came over from Massachusetts to cheer Mary up. Joseph too came down with flu but recovered more quickly than Mary, diverted from their personal loss by the demands of his crusade for tariff reform.

Highbury saw little of the Chamberlains that spring and early summer. Only Neville remained there. Austen and Joseph left for the opening of Parliament in

London. Austen's position as Chancellor kept him there and enforced his neutrality on tariff reform; the resulting estrangement from his father on this issue was felt by both men. Joseph too was kept away from his Birmingham base as he strove to rally the tariff reformers in Parliament in their deteriorating relationship with Balfour.

In this unhappy situation, the gardens and glasshouses of Highbury gave Joseph joy that he rarely found now in politics. Hilda Mary acted as a catalyst in this. He planned a garden for her, as Mary reported: '[With] six little paths a foot wide, a little seat to survey the six little borders, the whole enclosed in a little fence with a little gate, so she can shut herself in there. He is enchanted with the idea & so is she.' By Easter, 'Joe was in almost as much excitement as she was over the garden he has made for her & tore out to see that all was ready'.

His health had not, however, really recovered from the death of Ethel. He was in the throes of a migraine when he addressed his constituents in the Town Hall, and he struggled with the speech.

Like Joseph, Mary found solace in Highbury's garden. She arranged for terracing in a sheltered area where they could sit out whatever the weather, and they worked together on the garden whenever they could escape from London.

The tensions among Unionists reached crisis point towards the end of the year when the allied parties found themselves 'deep in the atmosphere of speeches'. Joe was eager for the fray in face of Balfour's determined resistance. Austen, on the contrary, was prostrated by the fight between the two men he most admired. Sciatica drove him to his bed upstairs in Highbury while down in the Library his father sat up until two or three in the morning preparing his battle cries. He used the Dining and Smoking rooms in Highbury to rally the leading forces for tariff reform locally and nationally. He forced a change in editor at the *Birmingham Daily Post* to bring it into line. He brought the leaders of the Conservative press nationally up from London to Highbury. William Hewins, now secretary of the Tariff Commission, came to report on his recent mission to Canada.

Balfour at last resigned as prime minister, none too soon for Chamberlain's liking; and a fresh general election was called for the beginning of the New Year, 1906. Joe plunged into the fray, drafting his election speeches, constantly writing letters and advising candidates. Mary and Ida had never previously felt any need to assist with electioneering – Hilda was out of the country – but went this time to rouse moral support from the still un-enfranchised women of Joe's constituency. Austen, however, remained bedridden even during the family's Christmas festivities, which were otherwise highlighted by the presence of Hilda Mary. Joe felt that Ethel was present when Hilda Mary was there. Nevertheless, before the day was out, he returned to work on his address to the Birmingham Jewellers' dinner at the end of the year when he would launch his election campaign.

Never was the importance to Chamberlain of his power base in Highbury so clearly demonstrated as in January 1906. He entered the general election believing that the Unionist defeat, which was only to be expected after a decade in power, could be reduced to survivable size. Concentrating on his Duchy, Joe sallied forth from Highbury every day to a different town in the West Midlands. With Austen returning only slowly to action, Neville took charge of all local organisation while Mary accompanied Joe everywhere, his constant companion and support.

General elections in those days spread out over several weeks. They began this time in Manchester, where the Liberals won every seat, including Balfour's. That result crushed Chamberlain's hopes for a speedy Unionist return to power. The Liberals seemed assured of a massive majority in the new Parliament and could remain in power beyond Joe's likely lifetime as he approached seventy.

Now uncertain of the results in his electoral Duchy, Chamberlain narrowed his campaign to Birmingham's seven seats. He was fairly confident of the six seats held by Liberal Unionists, but not about the seventh held by an ineffective Conservative. Birmingham went to the polls on 17 June. Joseph and Mary headed for the Town Hall where he voted. Then he drove all over the city in an open carriage, visiting almost every committee room.

Crowds gathered with mounting excitement around the Town Hall that evening when counting started. It began with Joe's seat for West Birmingham. Reversing the national trend, he carried it with a substantial increase over his massive victory in 1901. The other Liberal Unionist candidates followed suit. But they all waited anxiously for the result in Birmingham East – where the Conservative managed to survive. Hearing the erupting cheers from Highbury, Chamberlain telephoned his thanks to the crowd in words which were emblazoned on the Town Hall: 'Well done, Birmingham! My own people have justified my confidence, and I am deeply grateful to all who have assisted in winning this great victory. We are seven.'

Triumphant but exhausted, Chamberlain had thrown his all into this contest. Mary had to prompt him when he was lost for words, as happened with increasing frequency. The family had pleaded with him to ease up. But he refused: 'I cannot go half speed. I must either do my utmost or stop altogether and though I know the risks I prefer to take them.' His health was never the same afterwards. Still he refused to be daunted by the darkening political outlook or his deteriorating health.

The one brightening light occurred appropriately at Highbury but fell somewhat ironically on Austen. His health was still precarious when the election campaign began, and Beatrice was called in to rally moral support among the women of his constituency of East Worcestershire. Everyone in the family was relieved when he won re-election with a majority of Birmingham proportions. Highbury was part of his constituency; and it was to Highbury that a torch-bearing crowd came to cheer the result.

Afterwards Joseph was dogged by a succession of ailments: colds or flu, toothache, gout. When the new Parliament convened in London, he rallied the successful tariff reformers who formed a majority among the much-diminished ranks of elected Unionist MPs. With that reinforcement, Joe secured an ambiguous stalemate with Balfour who remained leader. All the Unionists welcomed the prolonged Easter recess as the new government settled in. Joseph and Mary headed for the Riviera, where Joe's gout returned, while Austen left for Algiers.

And it was there that he met, fell in love with, wooed and won the hand of Ivy Dundas – 'as quick about it as the Chamberlain men are', said Mary: 'Austen is as happy as the day is long – says he feels 25.' He was indeed rejuvenated. Ivy came from a family of military men and clergy, very different from the Chamberlains but right for the country gentleman that Austen was at heart. As the parliamentary recess came to an end, Mary welcomed Austen's fiancée and her family to Highbury.

Joseph, however, was preoccupied with the plans to celebrate his seventieth birthday and the thirtieth anniversary of his election to Parliament at the beginning of July. With

© Cadbury Research Library: Special Collections

Youngest daughter Ethel, with husband Whitmore Lionel Richards and daughter Hilda Mary.

© Cadbury Research Library: Special Collections

The Dutch Garden in springtime, one of the formal gardens at Highbury *c.* 1903.
Cattle from the hobby farm can be seen in the adjacent field.

© Illustrated London News Ltd/Mary Evans

© Birmingham Museums Trust

Torches lit the way as Chamberlain left Birmingham for his tour of South Africa in November 1902.

A torchlight parade was also a feature of Chamberlain's 70th birthday celebrations, where torch bearers received a commemorative medal.

© Illustrated London News Ltd/Mary Evans

© Cadbury Research Library: Special Collections

The 'two loaves' speech, prepared at Highbury, was effective in countering the 'big and little loaf' campaign of those opposed to tariff reform.

A devoted grandfather, Chamberlain designed a small garden of her own at Highbury for Hilda Mary.

© Cadbury Research Library: Special Collections

Leaving Highbury to tour the city on polling day for the 1906 election. All seven Liberal Unionist candidates were exceptional in resisting the swing to Liberals and Labour.

© Birmingham Museums Trust

Chamberlain resigned from government in September 1903 to fully devote himself to the nationwide campaign for tariff reform.

© Birmingham Museums Trust

Chamberlain's enduring popularity in Birmingham was evident at the celebrations to mark his 70th birthday and 30 years as M.P.

© Cadbury Research Library: Special Collections

Highbury garden parties were used to rally political support or celebrate achievements. In July 1913,
Austen Chamberlain marked 21 years as M.P. for East Worcestershire with his wife Ivy, son 'Little Joe' and stepmother Mary.

© Cadbury Research Library: Special Collections

Reproduced with permission of The Library of Birmingham, MS 4616 Box 17

DAILY SKETCH, MONDAY, JUNE 8, 1914.

Lady Blomfield Says No Insult To The King Was Intended.

DAILY SKETCH.

No. 1,637.   LONDON, MONDAY, JUNE 8, 1914.   [Registered as a Newspaper.]   ONE HALFPENNY.

CHAMBERLAIN MAKES HIS FIRST PUBLIC APPEARANCE FOR SEVEN YEARS TO ACKNOWLEDGE THE FAREWELL CHEERS OF HIS PEOPLE.

It was appropriate that Mr. Chamberlain's first public appearance since illness overtook him nearly eight years ago should have been at Highbury among his own people of West Birmingham, the constituency he has represented for so many years and which wanted to remain faithful to him always. When, to the surprise of everyone invited to the garden party held on Saturday at Mr. Chamberlain's residence, the veteran statesman, evidently in good spirits and looking bronzed and fairly well, was wheeled among his guests everyone cheered. They were delighted to see him amongst them again, though their pleasure was tinged with the regret that the meeting was something of a leave-taking as well as of a greeting. He waved his people good-bye, and with their cheers ringing in his ears and raising the old fire in his eyes he was wheeled back into the house again.—(Central News photograph.)

A fond farewell at a garden party to Chamberlain's devoted constituents after he had resolved not to stand again for election. This was his first public appearance in over seven years, but it was to be the last.

Serving a new purpose. The nursing staff and patients of the Highbury Auxiliary Hospital at the end of the First World War.

Reproduced with permission of The Library of Birmingham, MS 4616 Box 17

Once established as a war pensioners' hospital for wounded and disabled ex-servicemen, the glasshouses were replaced by pavilions for use as patient accommodation. They too were demolished by 1940 and replaced by Chamberlain House.

© Cadbury Research Library: Special Collections

The family reunited in 1934 for the opening of the Chamberlain Memorial Library (eldest daughter Beatrice had died in the influenza pandemic of 1918).
Front row L-R: Mrs Ann Chamberlain, Mrs Mary (Chamberlain) Carnegie, Neville Chamberlain, Lord Mayor, Sir Austen Chamberlain, Lady Mayoress, Lady Chamberlain, Ida Chamberlain, Hilda Chamberlain.

Reproduced with permission of the Library of Birmingham, WK/M6/259

Highbury becomes a home for elderly women but the Second World War brought male residents when their home was bombed. Communal areas and accommodation were moved to Chamberlain House.

Reproduced with permission of The Library of Birmingham, WK/K4.295

A view across Highbury Park in 1955. This public park was created in 1921 from 75 acres of the Highbury and Uffculme estates.

his encouragement the plans expanded to re-energise the political cause so close to his heart. After these celebrations in Birmingham he was to mobilise support nationally in a week of engagements in London with organisations supportive of tariff reform. The celebrations in Birmingham were to extend over a long weekend, moving on Saturday from a civic reception in the Council House to processions all over the city leading on Monday to Bingley Hall with a major address preceded by tributes from national and imperial institutions and ending with a torch-lit drive home to Highbury.

The celebrations began on Friday with festivities at all the educational institutions that Chamberlain had helped to found, including elementary schools from the 1870s and the University of Birmingham. Joe met with overwhelming enthusiasm at every stage in this near-royal progress.

Speaking on Saturday in the Council House to his colleagues of the past thirty to forty years, Joe summed up what he owed to the city: 'If I have been permitted to serve this community, no man has ever had more generous masters. They have been my teachers also. What I am for good or for ill, they have made me – this city of my adoption and of my affection.'

He was then driven amid cheering crowds through all the city parks. The poorer districts were particularly awash with garlanded colour, the crowds calling out: 'Good ol' Joe!' The festivities concluded at nightfall with fireworks in every park, ending with a dazzling pyrotechnic orchid that turned into a portrait of Joe.

On Monday evening thousands of men marching five-abreast to the call of 'Joe, Joe, Joe' lined the route to Bingley Hall where he addressed them. 'England without an empire', he declared prophetically, '… would be a fifth-rate nation, existing on the sufferance of its more powerful neighbours.' In the final analysis, however, his heart stayed at home. The prosperity of the nation would be insecure without cooperation between industrialists and labour. That had always been his message. The central objective of tariff reform as he saw it was to 'secure for the masses of the industrial population in this country constant employment at fair wages'.

His voice flagged towards the end of his speech. Sensing, perhaps half-hoping, that the words he spoke that night might be his last, he ended with a couplet:

'Others I doubt not, if not we,

The issue of our toil shall see.'

He was carried home that night on an elaborate river of fire. The torch bearers who lined his route swung in behind his carriage in waves separated by marching bands. The celebration ended with an ignited 900-square-foot 'Fire Portrait' of the incomparable leader.

He left the base of his power next day to take the afternoon train for the first of his meetings in London, this one with his Tariff Commission. He hurried on for tea with Mary in Prince's Gardens. There, after a hot bath, he was dressing for dinner when he suffered a stroke. He fell to the ground, his right side paralysed, but he remained fully conscious, aware of what had just happened.

Chapter Seven
STRICKEN

The stroke that brought Chamberlain down drained Highbury of much of its significance. Highbury had become a metaphor for the most dynamic person in the political life of Great Britain and its Empire. It was the house where Chamberlain made the weather. With almost symbolic significance he was stricken the day after he left Highbury for London.

But Highbury continued to figure at critical junctures in Chamberlain's remaining life. Even in his weakened condition, he – and hence Highbury – remained a focus of attention impossible – indeed dangerous – to ignore. Austen sustained that influence as his father's heir and the voice through which Joe's wishes were transmitted to the country. But there was a painful thread in this relationship between father and son. Though in appearance an almost photographic image of his father, no one mistook gentlemanly Austen for his aggressive father; and ardent tariff reformers yearned ever more fervently for Joe's leadership.

Mary's immediate concern was to obscure the extent of the stroke and sustain her husband's political influence. She sent her apologies for the dinner on the night of his stroke, saying that it was she who had taken ill. Joe's failure to appear at Austen's marriage a fortnight later gave the first indication of the seriousness of his setback. Not quite bedridden, he spent his days for the next month lying on the sofa in Prince's Garden's. Paralysed along his right side, he could neither speak intelligibly nor read and could walk only with great difficulty.

When Austen returned from honeymoon in September, Mary took Joseph back to Highbury, keeping him out of sight until their train reached Snow Hill station. The glimpse of him caught there in a bath chair strengthened suspicion that more was wrong with him than the family had let on. However, Highbury provided a congenial venue for rehabilitation away from prying eyes. The terrace in front of the house was a godsend: no longer a stage for speeches to the thousands, but a stretch for assisted walking, which he managed at increasing length. What worried him more, once

Parliament reconvened, was his inability to read and keep up with the news. Mary and Ida read to him for hours on end.

His removal from the centre of the political stage was now obvious, though the family continued to obscure the extent of his stroke. Austen returned to London, attempting to take charge of the campaign for tariff reform. He and Ivy found themselves a home there, and his possessions duly left Highbury. In November, under doctor's advice, Mary gave close members of the family permission to visit Joe. He found it extremely difficult for them to see him incapacitated.

Slowly, however, he began to recover. The stiffness on his right side eased and his speech improved. Although far from perfect, he joined in conversations at dinner. At the beginning of March Mary took him for further recovery to the French Riviera but there was no escape from recurrent gout that stopped his walking. When they returned to Highbury in June, Austen often came up from London to join them, leaving Ivy at Highbury when he had to return to London. And it was at Highbury in mid-October that Ivy gave birth to their first child, a son they called 'Little Joe'. It was a difficult birth, and Ivy stayed on at Highbury, strengthening its position as the family home.

The outlook for Highbury brightened unexpectedly that autumn when Balfour came to see Joe there in connection with a big meeting in Birmingham. Joe dreaded meeting anyone for the first time; and he was particularly apprehensive of meeting the leader of the Unionist Party with whom his relationship had been difficult for years. Stimulated, however, by the prospect, he recovered his powers of speech more than for quite a time, and the conversation revived his spirits. The two men talked about the issues in tariff reform that had divided them, particularly the tax on corn, and moved on to questions central to the debate with the Liberal government. Joe was surprised and heartened by the extent to which Balfour had come to agree with him. Mary was delighted by this reinvigoration of her husband, and she encouraged him to talk to other political associates. His speech, however, sometimes deteriorated during these encounters. And gout repeatedly set him back.

Before Christmas Hilda Mary returned to Highbury, bringing her father with her, and she joined Little Joe in an extended nursery. The whole family attended the christening of Little Joe at Kings Norton parish church a discreet distance away from

Highbury. Old Joe walked into the church by a back path from the vicarage and sat through the service. Hilda Mary helped distribute gifts at Christmas to the children of the Highbury gardeners. The demonstrative affection of the grandchildren warmed the old man's heart. He was also bolstered in the New Year by the improving fortunes of tariff reformers in parliamentary bye-elections.

Mary pulled him away from Highbury for a month's stay in Prince's Garden's at the opening of the parliamentary year. Joe went reluctantly, frustrated to be little more than an onlooker and uneasy about the encounters with colleagues that Mary kept arranging to strengthen his engagement. They left at the end of February 1908 for the restorative climate of the Villa Victoria near Cannes, their usual spring and early-summer home for the rest of Old Joe's life, and did not return to Highbury until the end of July.

He was always glad to return home, and did not want to leave Highbury even to visit sites in Birmingham in which he took pride. He was disheartened by medical treatments, particularly to his eyes, that drained his energy without improving his vision. Mary did her best to keep him from becoming a recluse. He was reluctant to see visitors, but she noted perhaps hopefully that his ability to converse was quickened by these visits. She insisted on his walking in the gardens whenever the weather permitted, and she induced him to read aloud every day to improve his speech. Pressing on, she took her still reluctant husband to London for three weeks late in the parliamentary year and brought him visitors almost daily. Beatrice and Neville did what they could to restrain Mary's pressure, but to little avail. Joe and Mary returned to Cannes for further medical treatments early in February 1909 and did not return to Highbury until the end of May.

The temperature of debate rose sharply after Lloyd George confronted Parliament with a budget that increased taxation on the landed rich in order to subvert the fiscal alternative, proposed by the Chamberlains, of heightened tariffs and imperial preference. That challenge brought Joe to London in July to rally his tariff reformers for the fight.

The centre of attention shifted back to Birmingham in September when Unionists massed for a demonstration to be addressed by Balfour as party leader. Special telephoning arrangements were made to transmit Balfour's speech to Chamberlain at Highbury. This marked the high point in their relationship. Balfour embraced tariff reform in terms that delighted Joe, as he told Balfour face to face next day at Highbury.

Joe returned to London in November to be on hand when the House of Lords rejected Lloyd George's budget. That rejection precipitated a constitutional crisis and the dissolution of Parliament for a general election in the New Year. Chamberlain threw everything that he still had into this fight. Gone was the reluctance to engage that he had displayed over the past three years. Highbury became the Unionist campaign centre for Birmingham and for the cause of tariff reform nationally. Austen conducted his campaign for re-election in East Worcestershire from Highbury. Neville plunged out farther into his father's electoral Duchy. Even Little Joe went around the house shouting '-tar 'orm!' for tariff reform.

But it was Old Joe himself who became the star of the show. Revealing the benefits of the medical treatments that Mary had induced him to undergo, he issued a manifesto to the press on 'The National Crisis'. He despatched columns of letters to tariff reforming candidates around the country, each one tailored to the particular candidate and constituency. Liberals feared the effect of these letters enough to spread the rumour that they could not possibly be the work of the stricken old man in Highbury.

The campaign also re-energised Austen since it brought together the two men he admired most in public life, his father and Balfour. However, the campaign quickly brought out the difference between them. Liberals appealed for popular support with a cry of 'The Peers versus the People', and Balfour responded by defending the House of Lords for rejecting Lloyd George's budget. But Old Joe recognised the popular appeal of the Liberal cry. He sought to focus the Unionist campaign instead on tariff reform with its promise to restore industrial production and employment.

They had contrived to ensure that Birmingham was polled on the first day of this election to set the pace for the country. Old Joe, unopposed in Birmingham West, was the first candidate to win election to the new Parliament. The other Unionist candidates for the city increased their margins of victory even beyond the results in 1906. And Unionists regained the dominance across the Duchy that they had lost last time.

Old Joe was, as usual, energised by the electoral campaign. Once the votes in Birmingham were tallied, he went to Moseley to cast his vote for Austen. News spread of the old man's arrival, and a large crowd shouted three cheers for him which he acknowledged 'in the old way' by leaning forward in his carriage to doff his hat. The voting for Austen in East Worcestershire held up well.

Again, however, the West Midlands were not representative of the rest of England. Although Unionists won as many seats as Liberals in the new House of Commons, the Liberals' return to power was assured by the support they received from Irish Nationalists and Labour.

Old Joe found these results more disheartening than the better ones in 1906. He could no longer see any hope for a speedy return to power until the Liberals lost their grip on the still prosperous textile manufacturing counties to the north. Sobered, he told a close lieutenant 'we shall have to wait our time and to move slower than we expected' – a discouraging prospect for a man of seventy-three in a wheelchair. After passing through London to record his election to the new Parliament, Joe travelled south to the Villa Victoria near Cannes. Although he resumed massage and electricity treatments there, his walking weakened and his speech deteriorated.

He returned home more than three months later. Highbury was no longer empowering. Joe found again and again in this eventful year that he had lost control of the political agenda. Highbury was no longer the house where the weather was made.

As he foresaw, the results of the January election took the wind out of tariff-reforming sails. The Liberal government's dependence on Irish Nationalist support in the Commons restored Home Rule in place of tariff reform as the centre of debate. And Unionists' reliance on their massive majority in the House of Lords to defeat Home Rule enabled the Liberals once again to raise their cry of 'The Peers versus the People', the cry that Chamberlain feared. On the eve of another general election precipitated at the end of the year by the impasse between the two Houses of Parliament over Lloyd George's budget, Balfour diluted the Unionist commitment to tariff reform.

The outcome of this second election of 1910 simply confirmed the first. Joe at Highbury sank further into depression of body as well as spirit. A recurrence of gout forced him into bed where he stayed over Christmas.

The pace of life at Highbury slowed down further in the New Year. During their prolonged sojourns on the French Riviera, the family had left Neville in charge of the house. His business interests kept him in Birmingham, as did his increasing involvement in the politics of the city. However, he found Highbury a desolate place on his own, exiled as he was to the upper floors with a skeleton staff and dust sheets over the central furniture. In the autumn of 1910 he fell in love with a young family connection, Annie Cole, a relationship that was quietly encouraged by his sisters. Now forty years of age, Neville was impatient to set up on his own. He and Annie found themselves a home in Edgbaston and arranged to be married in January. Old Joe, still immobilised, insisted that Mary attend the wedding without him. Afterwards, when they left again for Cannes, Highbury was divested of life.

The health of the old man continued to deteriorate at the Villa Victoria and turned still worse when they returned to Highbury. Simultaneously, the political temperature rose that summer when a Liberal bill to curb the power of the House of Lords reached the upper house. Always invigorated by a fight, Old Joe headed down to London to stiffen the resistance of the Unionist peers. He did so with a letter that deepened the division among Unionists between those he encouraged to fight to the bitter end and those led by Balfour who wanted a compromise in order to preserve the Lords' ability to fight another day.

When the compromisers prevailed, Joe retired from the fight. Back at Highbury he lapsed into lassitude of body if not of underlying spirit. Abandoning her efforts to sustain his political engagement, Mary protected him from potentially embarrassing face-to-face conversations, restricting dinner encounters to occasional events at the university and ensuring that Neville or other close male relatives were present to deflect attention from Old Joe's impairment.

The old man's spirits, and with them his health, improved in October when the voters of Canada rejected an attempt by their Liberal Government to embrace free trade with the United States instead of British imperial preference. He 'got back his speech',

Hilda reported in delight, '… quite distinct – even if not very fluent'. He was also invigorated by mounting calls for Balfour's resignation as leader of the Unionist Party. Through Neville, Old Joe called Austen, who was on holiday in Italy, to come home and take over.

Austen did as he was bidden, but his heart was not in it. He had none of the zest for a fight that invigorated his father. When it became clear that opposition to the Chamberlains from traditional Conservatives was too strong to overcome without a fight, Austen prevailed upon the Conservative candidate Walter Long to join him in withdrawing from the contest in favour of a third candidate, Bonar Law, who was acceptable to both sides.

Old Joe did not attempt to hide his disappointment with Austen. Joe admired Bonar Law's determination to fight for the leadership as well as his commitment to tariff reform. But the assault of the Liberal Government, with insistent support from the Irish Nationalists, on the powers of the House of Lords shifted the focus of debate away from tariff reform to Irish Home Rule which the Unionist majority in the Lords was determined to prevent. This shift eroded the commitment of most Unionists, including Bonar Law, to the tariff on imported wheat. However, Joe's vision of consolidating the Empire through tariffs depended on a British tariff preference for Canadian wheat. He spent the next year fighting to maintain that commitment.

When Bonar Law finally abandoned that commitment, the old man sensed that his years of political effectiveness had come to an end. Upon his return to Cannes, Joe told Mary that he would retire from Parliament at the next general election. Neither the Riviera nor his subsequent return to Highbury did anything to change his mind – or to arrest the deterioration in his health. The manifestations of gout spread to involve his eyes, intensified in his legs and clouded his voice. Mary all but abandoned her efforts to engage him in conversation with friends and former colleagues.

However, nothing could quite crush his will to fight. Back at Highbury in the autumn of 1913, he urged the fiercest resistance to Home Rule for Ireland, pressing beyond constitutional limits to the point of civil war. When Bonar Law and Sir Edward Carson, who were leading the resistance, came to Birmingham for a rally, Mary invited them to Highbury without much hope of anything further from Joe.

In fact, he sent them to the rally with a stark message: 'Hold fast and fight hard'. Mary thought he would have gone to bed when they returned from the rally. Instead she found him up awaiting his guests and joining them for a late supper and cigar.

In January 1914 Chamberlain gave the *Birmingham Daily Post* a letter announcing his resolve not to stand at the next general election. He wrote: 'I cannot hope again to do my work in Parliament.' May and he left almost immediately for the Riviera. They returned to England in the middle of May and to Highbury at the end of the month.

He invited his devoted constituents there to say goodbye on 6 June. Aside from glimpses as he was lifted in and out of trains, they had not seen him since his stroke nearly eight years previously. They were not sure that they would see him now. A reporter from *The Times* (8 June 1914) caught the moment:

> When it was reported that Mr. Chamberlain was on the terrace people hurried from all directions to pay their respects to him. He was seated in a bath chair. Every one was enabled to see Mr. Chamberlain as he was drawn backwards and forwards along the terrace in front of the house … Now and again there were little bursts of cheering which Mr. Chamberlain acknowledged by raising his hat, and as he passed along, men who had been in many a political fight with him bared their heads and shouted, 'Long life to you', and 'I wish we had you with us now'. Mr. Chamberlain smiled and shook his head and occasionally put out his hand, as he was wheeled about, to grasp that of some old political friend whom he recognized.

Before the speeches which Austen and others were to deliver, the old man 'turned to his guests, raised his hat … wished them good-night' and was wheeled back indoors.

He left Highbury for London for the last time on 19 June. Two weeks later he died. Highbury and the man who commissioned its construction had animated each other through good times and bad for thirty-five years. Now that Joseph Chamberlain had died, would Highbury fall into ruin? Or could it hold on to something of the spirit that had animated man and house for the past three-and-a-half decades?

Chapter Eight
RESTORING THE PURPOSE

The outlook for Highbury after Old Joe's death was bleak. Everyone in the family had left it by the end of the year. Austen and Neville already had homes elsewhere, Austen in London and Neville in Birmingham. Joe's will enabled his daughters to find homes for themselves elsewhere. They did so quickly, Beatrice near Austen in London, Ida and Hilda in the Hampshire village of Odiham with easy access to London.

Joseph left Highbury to Austen but otherwise made no provision in his will for the preservation of the house that had served him so well. After providing generously for the women in his family, he left his sons essentially to their own resources. Neville had prospered in business. By contrast, Austen had few business interests; his political involvements were financially rewarding only when he held office.

Mary was the only one in the family who could possibly have stayed on at Highbury had she wanted to. The Endicott family was much more affluent than the Chamberlains, even at Joe's richest. Mary had used 'gifts' from her parents to elevate the décor of her rooms at Highbury to her exacting taste. This parental money also paid for the annual sojourns on the Riviera after Joe's stroke. The maintenance of Highbury house and grounds would, however, have been a stretch even for Mary. And she did not want it, although she had loved the gardens. She had not warmed to Birmingham. The world she loved was of capital cities at the heart of national and international politics: Washington in her youth, London after marrying Joe. She had no desire to return to the United States, but she departed for Prince's Gardens in London as soon as she had dealt with Highbury.

She took charge of disposing of its contents to the houses in which Joe's children now made their homes. She found it a stressful business, 'every moment tugged at my heartstrings'. She despatched furniture to the new homes of her daughters-in-law, art to Austen, family china to Neville, the contents of the cellar to them all, silver to Prince's Gardens, gold plate to the bank. The garden ornaments from Highbury were distributed around the gardens of his children. Mary also had to find new positions for Highbury's long-loyal servants. By the beginning of December, the house stood empty. Joe's orchid collection was sold in London in April 1915.

The evacuation of Highbury was hastened because it had already found a function consonant with Joe's imperialism. The house and grounds provided excellent recovery space for troops wounded in the First World War. Highbury had proven its worth as a place for rehabilitation with Old Joe. The house was transformed in the early months of 1915 to open for wounded troops by May. Planned for 150 troops, Highbury offered further accommodation as their number soon exceeded expectation, and by the war's end it housed 240. The transformation of Highbury was designed initially for orthopaedic cases. However, when the war created new medical demands, facilities were developed for shell shock and nerve cases.

Relieved by this use of Highbury and soon preoccupied by increasing involvement in the governance of the country at war, Austen gave the house and the immediately surrounding land to the city. The Chamberlain family more broadly in Birmingham threw its support behind the use of Highbury for recovery of the wartime wounded. In addition to per patient financial support from central government, Kynochs – the armaments manufacturing company built up by Joseph's brother Arthur – provided much of the funding for the equipment and maintenance of Highbury as a hospital. And the women in the next generation of Arthur's family did volunteer work at the hospital and served on its general committee.

At the outset ten beds had been installed in the Dining Room, fourteen in the Drawing Room and six in Joseph Chamberlain's Library, while Austen's Smoking Room became an operating theatre. An open-air ward deemed essential for the treatment of chest wounds was established on the lawn opposite the front door. The Palm House and some of the glasshouses became wards. A large brick potting shed off the glasshouse corridor was converted into a gymnasium. The ornamental Dairy in the garden was altered to make it an isolation unit. In recognition of the need for rehabilitative acquisition of new skills or re-training in former ones, some glasshouses were equipped for metal work, shoe-making, tailoring, splint-making, typewriting and shorthand. The kitchen garden provided outdoor work in poultry and rabbit-keeping, gardening and growing fruit and vegetables.

Highbury met the wartime need well. And it went on doing so afterwards. Replacing the rest of the glasshouses, more wards were constructed to accommodate a total of 360 patients, and a specialist operating theatre and treatment rooms for orthopaedic cases were built. Highbury served eventually more than 12,000 of the wartime wounded. However, the number fell fast with recovery and departures in the late 1920s, and it was closed for this purpose in 1932.

Austen had assigned the house and surrounding land to the city in 1917. The arrangement was regularised in 1919 by the formation of a Trust for those in continuing need of care. The Trust Deed provided that if and when Highbury was no longer required for this purpose, the Trustees would retain it 'for the general benefit of the citizens of Birmingham'. This civic link was confirmed by the inclusion of the Lord Mayor as an ex-officio Trustee during his term of office.

With that broadening sense of purpose, the estate was reorganised and extended in the 1920s. Part was opened as a public park under the management of the city's Parks Committee. The rest was augmented by a bequest of land from the adjacent Cadbury estate of Uffculme and a further purchase by the Birmingham Civic Society recently founded by Neville Chamberlain, among others. Cricket pitches, football grounds, tennis and netball courts and a bowling green were established over the years for rental use by local clubs and schools. Refreshment stands, drinking fountains, public lavatories, a pavilion by the tennis courts and a shelter by the entrance drive were set up.

Highbury had served a national rather than a civic purpose since the death of Old Joe and the war. With the closure of Highbury as a military hospital in 1932, the Trustees made arrangements to place it and the surrounding gardens in the hands of the City Council, reinforcing its sense of civic purpose. At the same time the Trust strengthened the identification of Highbury with Chamberlain by restoring the Library to something of its former glory. The restoration was placed in the hands of the city's Museum and Art Gallery.

The family rallied to celebrate its opening, with Mary, Ida and Hilda returning to Highbury for the first time since 1914. Austen, in his address on the occasion, drew attention to his father's civic legacy: 'He with that splendid group of Birmingham citizens who took him for their leader made a new city on earth and, making this city of Birmingham and earning for it the title of the best-governed city of the world, they raised the dignity of municipal life far beyond the bounds of this city throughout the whole of the United Kingdom, and indeed, with repercussions beyond.' Hundreds visited the Library, now a museum, over the next few years.

The City Council assigned Highbury to its Public Assistance Committee for use as a home for aged women. In doing so the Council extended the civic vision of Joseph Chamberlain to embrace the more recent vision of Neville. As Minister of Health in the mid-1920s, Neville had laid foundations for the creation of a welfare state after the Second World War. The city in the 1930s funded the transformation of Highbury from a hospital for wounded soldiers into a home for the elderly. The temporary wards for wounded troops required improvement to protect the elderly particularly from the risk of fire. The women were moved into new wards out of the house so that it could provide centralised dining close to the kitchen.

This transformation proved disruptive and was barely completed when the Second World War broke out. The Library-museum was then closed. In 1940 when one of the homes for old men elsewhere in Birmingham was bombed, they were moved into Highbury. And the cultivation of vegetables to feed its ageing residents was extended beyond the kitchen garden into the flower beds.

Before the Library-museum was reopened after the war, Highbury underwent internal alterations to improve access for the public without encroaching on the privacy of the elderly residents. The centre of the house was repaired and redecorated. In 1970 Highbury received distinguished Grade II* listing.

However, all these renovations and improvements were expensive, far exceeding the income that Highbury generated. The financial estimates for 1970 placed the income from Highbury at £45,227 while the costs of maintaining it for the coming year were projected at £107,366. Even so, conditions in the rest of the house, including the rooms behind the gallery and the floors above it, were deteriorating.

By 1980 the cost of bringing Highbury up to the required standard for residential care of the elderly had risen alarmingly while the financial resources of the city had diminished and the thrust of public policy shifted towards care within the community. Highbury briefly became a day care centre before its closure as a residential home in 1982, at which time it reverted back to the City Council's General Purposes Committee.

Highbury found renewed life and purpose in the mid-1980s in connection with a programme of civic building supported by both parties in the Council. This initiative eventually gave Birmingham the Adrian Boult Hall, renovation of the Shakespeare Library and the International Convention Centre, including Symphony Hall. In this context, the General Purposes Committee assigned responsibility for civic catering to Highbury, roused by the ambition of the city's Chief Executive, Tom Caulcott, to turn it into the Birmingham equivalent of the Mansion House in London.

New light fittings in historic style were installed in the main rooms of the house along with restored carpets, curtains and furniture. Parking was provided at Highbury for the Lord Mayor to celebrate signal events in the city's calendar. He reopened the renovated house in 1985, renaming the Dining Room the Dorothy Lloyd Room after Joseph Chamberlain's granddaughter in her presence. A search for similar provision for royal visits to Birmingham was called off because of Highbury's proximity to a busy city road. Other organisations concerned with civic issues, such as the reconstituted Lunar Society, were encouraged to hold their meetings there. The general public were welcomed to the house on special opening days.

This rededication to civic purposes reached a climax in 1988 with a conference of people active in city planning, development, architecture and the arts. Convened at Highbury over a spring weekend, the conference came to be known as the Highbury Initiative. The question it confronted was how to transform the design quality of the city. Divided into groups, the attendees were bussed to different points on the Middle Ring Road and then walked back to Highbury to experience first-hand the existing quality of the city centre. They agreed that it was terrible. Hardly anyone lived there. Bumper-to-bumper buses and cars clogged New Street all day. The city centre was trapped in a concrete collar of elevated motorways over the wasteland beneath.

Shocked by what they had seen, the conference delegates regrouped in a number of workshops and plenary sessions, generating a series of principles and proposals for renovation. The organisers then drafted a set of policy documents. The full conference reconvened to review these recommendations. They reached several key conclusions: to pedestrianise the city centre to make it attractive socially as well as for business and shopping, to loosen the concrete collar by extending the heart of the city out from the Inner to the Middle Ring Road, to develop its distinctive districts like the Jewellery Quarter, and to raise the quality of design generally across the city. Two commissions were established, one under an American landscape architect to pedestrianise the city core – a plan that has since been extensively realised – and the second for an urban designer to draw up a policy for the city centre, a plan now evident in the surface-level layout of Moor Street.

The Highbury Initiative took effect gradually, with setbacks as well as advances, through the 1990s into the twenty-first century. It provided one more expression of the Civic Gospel that inspired Joseph Chamberlain in the 1870s to turn Birmingham into a model of urban regeneration.

However, the Highbury Initiative was soon followed by rising concerns within the regulatory Charity Commission about the city's management of Highbury. The City Council's assignment of Highbury for catering had lost its sense of civic purpose. It provided hospitality and occasional banquets for social, political and cultural organisations in Birmingham, and it developed a lucrative business as a venue for weddings. The revenue from these services, however, went into City Council coffers without being earmarked for maintenance and renovation of the estate. The restoration in the mid-1980s was confined to the ground floor and around the gallery. Catering ignored the rest of the house, which continued to deteriorate while the costs of maintenance, let alone restoration, continued to mount.

The public park beyond the house, although under different civic administration, found itself suffering from similar neglect by the beginning of the twenty-first century. The park had been well managed after the Second World War with a staff of fifteen gardeners and two parks policemen on bicycles. It was opened for garden fêtes, marquees were provided with a water supply, fencing and entrance pay boxes were installed. The park was especially busy in the 1970s with fêtes for local organisations, scout groups, boys' clubs and the CND. But activity fell off in the last quarter of the twentieth century alongside the depression in the city's manufacturing base. With funding from the city accordingly reduced and vandalism rising, sports grounds, drinking fountains, lavatories and refreshment stands fell into disuse and were demolished.

Although there was one attempt to improve the park in connection with the Queen's Ruby Jubilee in 1992, it was ill-considered. Disregarding pleas from the Garden History Society and the park's inclusion in the English Heritage Register of Parks and Gardens of Special Historic Interest, an extensive arboretum was planted at its heart. It greatly reduced the area of open space, damaged the historic character of the meadowlands, and raised the cost of restoring the park to anything like its former glory.

What was happening to the park added to the concern about what was happening to the house. Was the City Council using Highbury for the benefit of the citizens of Birmingham, as required by the Trust of 1919 and 1932? Was it even keeping Highbury in adequate repair? Under the terms of the Trust, the City Council was in effect sole trustee of Highbury. How, legally, could the City Council defend its right to be sole trustee and be at the same time sole beneficiary of the Trust? What was the City Council doing to meet its charitable obligations?

These questions raised alarm in the Moseley community around Highbury. Meanwhile the City Council grew concerned at the mounting costs of maintaining the Highbury estate after years of neglect, a concern exacerbated by a threat from the Charity Commission to penalise the City Council for failure to meet its charitable obligations.

These concerns reached boiling point in 2009 after the City Council proposed to meet its financial obligations at Highbury by selling some of the outlying buildings. That proposal provoked Tony Thapar of the Moseley Community Development Trust to protest that the City Council, '… as both landlord and tenant, had a clear conflict of interest. How could it be the sole trustee and then sell the assets to generate funding for itself?'

A Highbury Coalition took shape, including the Kings Heath Forum and the Friends of Highbury Park. Mary de Vere Taylor, Joseph Chamberlain's great-great-granddaughter, threw herself into the effort. She complained with some of the eloquence of her forebear at the failure of the City Council to satisfy the demands of the Charity Commission for a meeting of the concerned public. She added the voice of her family to the local demands for the creation of an independent trust to take charge of Highbury. The City Council's Trusts and Charities Committee responded testily.

At last in 2016, in line with the demands of the protestors, and consonant with the Civic Gospel that inspired the construction of Highbury in the first place, a new Chamberlain Highbury Trust was set up to seek funding and take charge to restore the estate for the general benefit of the citizens of Birmingham. The new Trust brought together city planners, experts on the history of the estate, business interests and local leaders. They drew up both aspirational and concrete objectives to open the house to the public on a permanent basis with a tea room and dedicated conference and teaching facilities. Plans were developed to restore house and grounds to their former glory. Open days for the public were reinstituted and attracted substantial crowds.

The new Trust hopes to use the estate to inspire the younger generation to develop the leadership skills that the Chamberlains displayed from the mid-nineteenth to the mid-twentieth century and to bring the now diverse communities in Birmingham closer together. Already students from the nearby academy named after Joseph Chamberlain have visited the house. They came well prepared with questions about its former residents, inspired by their achievements and excited by the persisting grandeur of the house. Then they frolicked outside, girls in head-scarves cartwheeling enthusiastically over its grassy terrace.

Bibliography and Sources

This book draws heavily on the published and unpublished sources listed below, supplemented with research into a variety of archival sources about Highbury, its architecture and landscape, the use of the house and grounds over time, and some of the people who lived and worked there. The consulted sources also include some suggested reading which may prove useful to anyone wishing to explore in more detail about Highbury.

Archive Sources

The Chamberlain Collection is held at the Cadbury Research Library, Special Collections at the University of Birmingham. This rich collection is divided into the political and private papers of individual family members (References: JC, AC, BC and NC) and also the Chamberlain Family Collection (Reference: C), which for this publication, has been invaluable for photographs, diaries, visitor books and magazine articles. Perhaps the most illuminating source about the Chamberlains' life at Highbury is the vast collection of letters written by Mary Endicott Chamberlain to her mother in America (they can be found in the papers of Austen Chamberlain, Reference: AC4/3).

Other archive sources relevant to the period after the Chamberlains are held at the Library of Birmingham. They include photographs, pamphlets and minute books for the auxiliary and war pensioners' hospital and Home for Aged Women. (BCC1/BW – Birmingham Pensions Hospitals; L34.3 Birmingham Council Proceedings; MS 4616 Box 17 WWI Hospitals; MS 554 – Records of Highbury Hospital; MS 995 Lord Mayor's Fund for Relief of Disabled Soldiers and Sailors).

Published Works

Ballard, P., "'Rus in Urbe': Joseph Chamberlain's Gardens at Highbury, Moor Green, Birmingham 1879-1914', *Garden History,* Vol. 14 (1), 1986, pp. 61-76.

Ballard, P., *Highbury Park, Moseley Birmingham: Historic Landscape Appraisal* (Birmingham City Council, 2009).

Chamberlain, A., *Politics from Inside: An Epistolary Chronicle 1906-1914* (Cassell and Co. Ltd, London, 1936).

Churchill, W. S. *Great Contemporaries* (Readers Union/Thornton Butterworth, London,1939).

Holyoake, J., 'John Henry Chamberlain' in P. Ballard (ed.) *Birmingham's Victorian and Edwardian Architects* (Oblong/Victorian Society, Wetherby, 2009).

Hunt, T., *Building Jerusalem: The Rise and Fall of the Victorian City* (Weidenfeld and Nicolson, London, 2004).

MacKenzie, N. and J. (eds.) *The Diary of Beatrice Webb, Vol. I 1873-1892* (Virago Press Ltd, London, 1982).

Marsh, P. T., *Joseph Chamberlain: Entrepreneur in Politics* (Yale University Press, London, 1994).

Marsh, P. T., *The Chamberlain Litany: Letters Within a Governing Family from Empire to Appeasement* (Haus Books, London, 2010).

Reekes, A., *Two Titans, One City: Joseph Chamberlain and George Cadbury* (History West Midlands, Alcester, 2017).

Reekes, A., *The Birmingham Political Machine: Winning Elections for Joseph Chamberlain* (History West Midlands, Alcester, 2018).

Rice, C. (ed.), *Highbury: A Brief History and Guide* (History West Midlands, Alcester, 2018).

Roberts, Sian. (with the Library of Birmingham), *Birmingham: Remembering 1914-18* (The History Press, Stroud, 2014).

Roberts, Stephen., *Joseph Chamberlain's Highbury: A Very Public Private House* (Birmingham Biographies, Birmingham, 2015).

Whitehill Laing, D., *Mistress of Herself* (Barre, Massachusetts, 1965).

Newspapers and Periodicals

Birmingham Daily Post
Daily Mail
London Illustrated News
Manchester Guardian
Punch
The Times

Unpublished Sources

Ballard, P., 'A Commercial and Industrial Elite: A Study of Birmingham's Upper Middle Class, 1780-1914', Unpublished PhD thesis, University of Reading (1983).

Chamberlain Highbury Trust, 'CHT Landscape History 1878-Present and Restoration Proposals' (unpublished, 2018).

Online Resources

McGough, L. and Thomas E., *Delivering Change: Putting city centres at the heart of the local economy (2014)*, www.centreforcities.org

Index

Note: page references in italics indicate images.